Thomas Berry

A Book of Hours

We come here to begin to relieve an ancient wrong.
We wish especially to restore to this Earth its ancient joy.
For while much of what we have done is beyond healing,
there is a resilience throughout the land
that only awaits its opportunity to flourish once again
with something of its ancient splendor.
Thomas Berry

Thomas Berry

A Book of Hours

Edited by
Kathleen Deignan, CND

ORBIS BOOKS
Maryknoll, New York 10545

Library of Congress Cataloging-in-Publication Data

Names: Berry, Thomas, 1914-2009, author. | Deignan, Kathleen, 1947- editor.
Title: Thomas Berry : a book of hours / edited by Kathleen Deignan.
Description: Maryknoll, NY : Orbis Books, [2025] | Includes bibliographical
   references.
Identifiers: LCCN 2024039905 (print) | LCCN 2024039906 (ebook) | ISBN
   9781626985995 (trade paperback) | ISBN 9798888660546 (epub)
Subjects: LCSH: Berry, Thomas, 1914-2009. | Ecotheology—Catholic Church. |
   Books of hours. | Breviaries.
Classification: LCC BX4705.B4455 B47 2025 (print) | LCC BX4705.B4455
   (ebook) | DDC 261.8/8—dc23/eng/20241120
LC record available at https://lccn.loc.gov/2024039905
LC ebook record available at https://lccn.loc.gov/2024039906

This Book of Hours is dedicated to the peerless spiritual guide and lover of the Living Earth

Thomas Berry

and to the Ecozoic family he has called to undertake The Great Work for the healing of our Common Home—

All Berry Kin, a growing circle of community and commitment.

Contents

Acknowledgments   *xi*

Shining Forth: Thomas Berry,
   Spiritual Master of the Ecozoic   *xv*

Prologue: "The Meadow Across the Creek"   *xxxiii*
   by Thomas Berry

Sunday
A New Story

Dawn ~   3
Day   ~   11
Dusk ~   17
Dark ~   25

Monday
The Mystery of Meadow

Dawn ~   31
Day   ~   38

Dusk ~ 45
Dark ~ 53

Tuesday
The Human Venture

Dawn ~ 59
Day ~ 65
Dusk ~ 71
Dark ~ 79

Wednesday
A Communion of Subjects

Dawn ~ 85
Day ~ 92
Dusk ~ 99
Dark ~ 106

Thursday
The Great Work

Dawn ~ 113
Day ~ 119
Dusk ~ 125
Dark ~ 131

Friday
Desolation and Destiny

Dawn ~ 139
Day ~ 145

Dusk ~ 152
Dark ~ 161

Saturday
Pax Gaia

Dawn ~ 169
Day ~ 176
Dusk ~ 182
Dark ~ 189

Sunday II
Toward the Ecozoic

Dawn ~ 197
Day ~ 203
Dusk ~ 209
Dark ~ 216

Final Benediction   223

Postscript   225

Abbreviations   227

References   229

Bibliography and Permissions   247

Acknowledgments

With gratitude for those who have become "Berry Kin" these many decades of collaboration in the Great Work. Though the list is endless, these are to me in time most long-standing, in space most proximate, and so my thanks:

To the Co-Founders of the Berry Forum for Ecological Dialogue, faithful friends and brothers, each and all: Danny Martin, Brian Brown, and Kevin Cawley.

And to the wider circle of Berrians, inspiring colleagues and companions: Mary Evelyn Tucker, John Grim, Francesco Gargani, James Robinson, Scott Thompson, Anthony Mullen, Brian Swimme, Vaughn Fayle, Kathy Duffy, Joe Holland, Fletcher Harper and GreenFaith Fellows, Monica Hoyt, Green Mountain Monastery Sisters, Berry Contemplative Ecologists, Carl and Elena Procario-Foley, Liam Myers, Sam King, and the beloved Iona Faculty of Religious Studies, then and now.

Always thanks for the support of my Congregation of Notre Dame Sisters and Associates who have made the Great Work a solemn vocation, especially Libby Osgood, CND, for her generosity of time and skill during her own writing sabbatical.

For the blessings of my wonderful Iona colleagues: the inspiring teaching scholars of the Faculty of Religious Studies, my counselors Marie Pace and Joseph Stabile, and all my Iona colleagues who teach the New Story and serve the Great Work.

To Peggy Healy for her bounty of bread and roses, and to Joseph Madonna for his careful reading of my drafts.

Most especially to my sister Ann Deignan, for her keen literary eye surveying this manuscript and her loving infusion of affirmation all throughout. Her life of care for the gardens and woodlands she protects and her fierce sense of justice for the vulnerable of this planet is an anticipatory flowering of the *Ecozoic* we work and pray to become.

And for the sweet companionship of Neenie and Sophie, two feline friends who lived and passed with me during the creation of this work.

My final tribute is offered to Iona University student Layne McDonald, first recipient of the Dr. Ann Deignan Earth and Spirit Internship Award. An aspiring environmental lawyer currently majoring in biology/ecology, Layne's partnership in bringing this Berrian Book of Hours to realization over an academic year of countless hours of discovery was a daily blessing for us both. May Thomas Berry continue to inspire her life of Earth advocacy.

And a blessing for my thousands of students near and far, especially the young Berry scholars who served the Deignan Institute for Earth and Spirit in their time: Christopher O'Connor, Sharon Terry, Peggy Clark, Joseph Madonna, Layne McDonald, Ceire Kealty, Dan and Kimberly Potocki, Jamal Jackson, Christine Samwaroo, Connor Murray, Lazar Paroski, Francesca Boyer, Gabriel and Danielle Cabrales, Rick

Palladino, Promise Jiminez, Ashley Hubaykah, Ashley Rose, Legrand Beauvais, Louis Ramos, Harley Cheko, Keegan Boison Yeats, Kayla Edwards, Kyle Byrne, Anna Kearney, Robert Droel, Jasmin Ruffin, John Martinez, Jiya Dorcas Greene, Anthony Ostrovsky, Sandybell Anorga—and countless more with more to come.

Shining Forth

Thomas Berry
Spiritual Master of the Ecozoic

*In the name of
the Universe,
the Earth,
and the Human—
all centered in one another.*

It is a joy to offer you the blessing of this *Book of Hours*, a labor of love and gratitude to honor and magnify the inspired wisdom of Thomas Berry, one of the most lucent planetary thinkers of our time and a singular spiritual master for this season of peril and promise. This is the third and last of a trilogy of contemporary breviaries created for contemplatives of our moment and for our moment—an indescribable moment of global upheaval for all beings who comprise the commune of this living Earth. Ours is an era of both evolutionary and revolutionary transmutations affecting every facet of terrestrial life.

We cosmic pilgrims are making our way on a heroic journey in an ineffable, still-unfolding universe toward a destiny both unknown and unimaginable. For such a hazardous adventure we need guides of all sorts. Most especially, we need spiritual guides—sages and shamans, mystics and mentors—to shine forth and illuminate the way before us with their hard-won and divinely inspired wisdom.

Three such luminaries have bequeathed their insight and foresight in language wonderfully original to each, that has become a new vocabulary for prayer: Thomas Merton, the monastic master who explored the wilderness of the modern human soul; Pierre Teilhard de Chardin, the visionary scientist who explored the deep-time wilderness of the cosmos; and here, Thomas Berry, the "geologian" and ecological prophet who explored the vibrant though vanishing wilderness of the living Earth, newly comprehended and now most critically compromised. Each was a priest within and beyond their shared Catholic tradition; each a sophisticated postmodern worldling of the twentieth and twenty-first centuries; each a prophet announcing the true state of affairs of the human person within the body of humankind, the body of Earth, the body of cosmos, the body of divinity. Each remains a sage given to us, speaking to us in his own elegant poetics of the spirit. Each is a spiritual master to whom we owe a debt of immense gratitude, and so to each his *Book of Hours*.

Encouraged by the generous reception of the Merton and Teilhard breviaries, I offer this creative endeavor to honor in a special way my own teacher and spiritual master, Father

Thomas Berry. The blessing of his mentorship continues to shine forth in my life and summons me to engage with you in the "Great Work" of Earth-healing and integral ecological education. It is my hope that your encounter with him during the hours of your daily meditation may likewise be a blessing bestowed through his luminous language. May it become a new vocabulary of *Ecozoic* prayer, as Thomas opens for you the doors to the "house of life" shining forth at dawn, at day, at dusk, and at dark.

MEETING THE MASTER OF ECOZOIC SPIRITUALITY

It would require another book all its own to recall Thomas Berry's exceptional life. Fortunately, that refined biography has been wonderfully realized by his beloved students, Mary Evelyn Tucker and John Grim, primary lineage bearers and custodians of his intellectual estate. To these remarkable scholars and ecological pioneers a salute of gratitude not simply for aiding in the realization of Thomas's trove of publications but also for taking his legacy into every zone of this planet with other Berry legates, most notably mathematical cosmologist Brian Swimme. With their film, *Journey of the Universe*, and courses offered through Coursera, they have created and continue to curate a dynamic and expanding virtual theater of encounter with Thomas on vibrant websites that offer access to the archive of his life and works in every medium. May you find your way to them, and find in them an opening to a new world of awareness and continuing Berrian education.

MOMENTS OF GRACE

*A magic moment gave my life something
that seems to explain my life at a more profound level
than almost any other experience I can remember.*

Thomas was blessed by what he called "moments of grace" that marked a life that unfolded over the arc of the twentieth century from 1914–2009. Born William Nathan Berry, he was one of thirteen children fortunate to have been raised in the still rich, rural world of the southern meadows and streams of North Carolina. When he was twelve years old, as reported in the Prologue, he had a defining moment of grace while ambling alone in a meadow, an Earth epiphany in a field of lilies that remained the touchstone for his life. It was a fleeting instant of rapture in the numinous beauty shining forth in the wilderness, a moment of grace that remained an inner illumination lighting his way throughout his life. But that spell also awakened in him an early sense of ecological foreboding that an industrial juggernaut was targeting the vitality of his living world. Early on he sought refuge from the disfiguring development implied by such commercial order. With concern over the rapidity of social and technological change bearing down on his precious wilderness, he reports intuitively knowing his need for a special environment to support his "brooding" creativity. Thinking that only jail or a monastery would provide the contemplative quarters he desired, he opted for the neighboring Passionist Order, which he entered at the age of thirteen. In that moment of grace he both found a new home and was given a new name: Thomas, after Aquinas, honoring the great theologian who would become his intellectual inspiration and mentor. Among his Passionist brothers he was ordained to bear a charism that would set his life in accord with a divine passion playing itself out, not only in human history, but as he would discover, throughout the ever-unfolding cosmos.

Tell us not about the Passion of Christ in ancient times,
but about the Passion of Earth in our times.

A historian by nature, Thomas pursued graduate studies to refine his highly intuitive comprehension of the designs and dynamics of human affairs. After completing his doctorate in the history of Western thought at the Catholic University of America, he went to China to undertake Asian studies. There another fortuitous moment of grace afforded what became a lifelong friendship with the renowned Asian scholar Theodore de Bary, who deepened Thomas's appreciation for Eastern traditions, particularly Confucianism. Returning to the States, they engaged together in scholarly collaborations that oriented Thomas toward his own recognition as an exceptional interpreter of the religious cultures of humankind.

In the 1960s another moment of grace radicalized his sense of history: his engagement with the writings of Pierre Teilhard de Chardin. The Jesuit paleontologist turned theo-cosmologist gave Thomas the grand vision of a more comprehensive sacred story, the unfolding of the universe in an enigmatic cosmogenesis of inscrutable complexity. With the liberating expanse of this "new scientific story" Thomas's mind was no longer confined within human or terrestrial histories. His vision stretched toward a cosmic horizon as his attention shifted toward the "shining forth" of time itself and of all phenomenal existence secretly enfolded within it.

The epic of evolution.
The story of the universe.
This is our sacred story.
The ultimate mystery whence all things come into being.

With rare linguistic precision and eloquence Thomas wove the wisdom of evolutionary science with the wisdom of ancient classical traditions. At the same time he brought to the center of his discourse the marginalized wisdoms of women and Indigenous peoples, who held for him modes of knowing critical for the full telling of the new revelatory story. Thomas presented his multifaceted curriculum in a unique graduate program in the History of Religions at Fordham University, enriched by his innovative programming at the Riverdale Center of Religious Research. There he mentored a new generation of religious thinkers to comprehend the power and purpose of religious creativity.

In his mature years Thomas wrote and traveled far and wide to tell the new story of the sacred universe and our role in it. But his teaching presented more than the mysteries of a sacred universe straining toward intelligibility through the human species. It also announced the unfolding catastrophe confronting our singular planet at the hands of the same human species entrusted with its care and protection. As Thomas sang the glories of this still-becoming universe, he lamented the desolation of our once-in-a-cosmos living home.

In his elderhood Thomas embodied his own peripatetic mode of teaching sacred Earth studies; he had truly found his venerable voice. To his students, his audiences, and his disciples, he sounded a prophetic keynote to announce in his own poetics a unique vision and grand proposal. "The New Story" and "The Great Work" name the inclusive categories through which he articulated in elegant detail a manifesto for the revival of a flourishing Earth community set in its evolutionary context. Thomas had established his teaching chair not only in the academy and other forums of erudition, but more originally and organically under a great oak tree on the banks of the Hudson River, where he contemplatively attended the hours of his days. The boy of the meadow had become a prophet for the planet.

> *We need the guidance of the prophet,*
> *the priest, the saint, the yogi,*
> *the Buddhist monk, the Chinese sage,*
> *the Greek philosopher, and the modern scientists.*
> *We need an ecological spirituality*
> *with an integral ecologist to serve as spiritual guide*
> *for these times.*

As with our ancestors through the long ages of our evolution, present human society needs its seers and shamans to guide us through peril and awaken us to meaning and the promise of flourishing survival. Thankfully, they arise in our midst and offer us their light so we might proceed toward life-enhancing modes of existence. But this time is like no other time, as we know. This time is in fact the end-time for the splendid "Cenozoic Age" of Earth's flourishing—the past 67 million years of unrepeatable biodiversity and geologic stability. As Thomas lamented, that is all passing now, and what we are passing into is yet to be seen. But the seer sees, and Thomas was a seer.

It is difficult simply to identify the multidimensional reality that Thomas saw. It is also a challenge to give a valid name to the seer. Neither scientist nor theologian and more than a religious historian, he named himself a *geologian*—one who comprehended and would tell the Earth story in all its myriad splendor and spoilage. But Thomas was not merely a descriptive scholar, he was more truly a prescriptive cultural therapist, and his prescription for the human community of the twenty-first century addressed the root of our crisis and offered a route to our healing.

An Ecozoic Vision

*The Cenozoic Era in the story of Earth is fading
as the sunset in the western sky.
Our hope for the future
is for a new dawn, an Ecozoic Era,
when humans will be present to the Earth
in a mutually enhancing manner.*

Our ancestors gave birth to the power and purpose of human religion in response to their confrontation with the mystery and terror of existence in an unfathomable universe. Religions, as Thomas taught, were themselves cosmic and psychic power systems channeled through diverse vessels of cultural complexity and creativity. Yet however much Thomas affirmed the constructive potentials of traditional religious forms, he saw with prescience the need for a new "meta-religious" movement in this accelerating time of evolutionary advancement and planetary plunder. While it remains for each religion to make its particular ecological contribution to this moment of Earth history, neither any one nor all together can supply the sustaining psychic energy required by the human community during this critical age of struggle for ecological survival. A new religious modality is necessary to respond to the ongoing revelations of the sciences that at once present a model of our unitive cosmos, still in genesis, and an indisputable assessment of the accelerating disintegration of our living planet. More so, an Ecozoic mode of religious consciousness was necessary to articulate the evolutionary meaning of this moment.

Thomas named his vision of such a new moment of planetary history the *Ecozoic*—a new era when our living house might once again be the home of vibrant, flourishing vitality in the aftermath of an age of human desecration. He understood that a compelling and inspiring vision of the future was necessary to give hope and orientation to those tasked with generating the new conditions for a sustainable Earth. He was confident that the *Ecozoic* could be born, if we labored to birth it. Paradoxically, the *Ecozoic* could only be born if the human species rebirthed or "reinvented" itself as a creative participant in the great commune of creation. This is the essential labor of "The Great Work" that Thomas explicitly detailed as the way forward for our human generations, a monumental task that would last for the ages required to restore a new mode of viability to our living Earth. The duration for this work he calculated not in decades but in millennia; though it took but a few centuries to unravel the perfectly calibrated conditions for a living Earth, it originally took 13.8 billion years to establish them. Clearly, such a heroic endeavor of restoration will demand great stores of human energy and a spirituality to sustain it. We are grateful that Thomas had a vision for that too.

We need a spirituality that emerges out
of a reality deeper than ourselves,
a spirituality that is as deep as the Earth process itself,
a spirituality born out of the solar system
and even out of the heavens beyond the solar system.
For it is in the stars that the primordial elements
take shape
in both their physical and psychic aspects.

Ecozoic Spirituality

Long before others proposed the contours of an ecological spirituality, Thomas comprehended the true dimensions and authentic orientations of such transformative practice. He noted the hubris of attempts to compose an eco-spirituality that simply reveres nature as missing the point entirely, since this would only strengthen our human habit of objectifying the natural world as another "other," however venerable. He exhorts us rather to surrender our anthropocentric narcissism and humbly enter as one of the inestimable "Earthlings" into mutual, benevolent relationship with the multifaceted being of the living Earth itself. Thomas did not promote a spirituality about the Earth, but a way of awakening to Earth's own mysterious spiritual life—Earth as original subject generating our existence, our mother, teacher, and healer, our primordial spiritual activator. In such daring relationship with the maternal mystery of Gaia the human has a chance to be reborn. This was the singular requirement for the healing of our planet. Since the present modality of human nature is too compromised and conditioned in self-centeredness to bring forth the *Ecozoic*, a new kind of humankind must evolve under the pressure of its own conscious exertion. Indeed, such rebirthing of our species—by our own will and labor—is the first objective of the "Great Work" to be done:

> *The historical mission of our times*
> *is to reinvent the human—*
> *at the species level,*
> *with critical reflection,*
> *within the community of life-systems,*
> *in a time-developmental context,*
> *by means of story and shared dream experience.*

With penetrating insight, Thomas perceived our primordial affliction to be rooted in rage against the pervasive agony of the human condition itself. It is, essentially, our refusal to accept the conditions under which life is given. The enterprise of past civilizations could be understood as the human effort to divorce our species from the matrix of the natural world, thus releasing us from its demands and discipline. In our time technological sophistication and its manipulations have overwhelmed our sense of enmeshment within a living web of beings. We have objectified ourselves as other than all others. Such isolation is supported by our machines, to which we are addicted, and by which we are enslaved in Thomas's mind, we have fallen into a technological trance, the sleep of the machine, which obscures any palpable sense of dependency on each and every other kind who with us are resident in an organic biocracy. Other beings are addressed as commodities for our utility and commerce rather than as relatives and essential contributors to the survival of the whole.

The irony of course is that the cost of our splendid achievements in the modern period to build an alternative wonder world has come due in the desecration of our own life-support systems. In a stunning summary of our predicament Thomas reminds us: *the glory of the human has become the desolation of Earth, and the desolation of Earth is becoming the destiny of the human.* The "Great Work" of our present and future generations is to meet with vision and vigor the threats to the survival of the living biome. Clearly there is an urgency in the task of human transformation on all frontiers of our existence since only those sufficiently awake and aware will be empowered to bring the new humanity forward.

Our challenge is to create a new language,
a new sense of what it is to be human.
It is to transcend not only national limitations,
but even our species isolation,
to enter into the larger community of living species.
This brings about a completely new sense
of reality and of value.

Thomas's "Great Work" has been to map our coordinates in this unprecedented Earth moment and open possible routes toward a new era of survival. In this regard, his comprehensive legacy is rightly studied in institutes of education from kindergarten to university. But Thomas lives on with us not simply as a peerless religious historian; he abides with us more personally and intimately as a spiritual master for our generations. It is the intention of this Berrian *Book of Hours* to make present and accessible the wisdom of an Ecozoic Sage offering his transforming insight to heal, nurture, enlighten, and guide us through our glorious and perilous Anthropocene days.

Praying the Hours with Thomas Berry

Thomas Berry never composed a breviary for the new humans in gestation, whom he meant to nurture. He never privileged one kind of spiritual practice over another. Rather, he asked us to sidestep immature modes of eco-piety and theologizing so that a more sensitive and somber practice of silence would sensitize us to the prayer of the planet. Though Thomas never wrote prayers or psalms per se, it has been a protracted interval of grace for me to discover in the richness of his written legacy, a trove of glorious hymns, canticles, litanies, and blessings to revive our Ecozoan soul and senses.

When you come to prayer on the First Sunday of your Ecozoic contemplation, Thomas begins his sacred telling of the *"New Story"* of our cosmos as epic, as prophecy, as gospel.

> *The universe is*
> *the primary revelation of the divine,*
> *the primary scripture,*
> *the primary locus of divine-human communion.*

At dawn he awakens the quiet memory of our origins in the primordial flaring forth of the mystery that Berrian poet Drew Dellinger described as *"The Secret One slowly growing a body."* As you move into your day, you are invited to more deeply remember the story of your becoming, then again at dusk, and again at dark.

Monday calls us into *"The Mystery of the Meadow"* where with young Thomas we might recover our child's mind in the discovery of a numinous world of subtle intelligibility shining forth in the sensuous beauty of living forms. At the Day hour we are met with a gentle exhortation: undergo re-enchantment with the Earth, for this is the necessary condition for our rescue of the Earth from the impending destruction that we are imposing upon it.

Tuesday invites our engagement with the challenge and seriousness of *"The Human Venture"* in a day of contemplative realignment with our true nature as a species ordained for a profound service to the cosmos. In an affirming doxology Thomas reminds us that humans and the universe were made for each other.

> *The Universe,*
> *the Earth,*
> *and the Human*
> *are centered in one another.*

At Dusk on Wednesday our prayer brings us into *"A Communion of Subjects"* to move us beyond anthropocentric democracy to ecological biocracy in joyous participation with the larger life community. With Thomas we sing a hymn to "appreciate the dazzling wonder of the sacred dimension that finds expression in the universe itself," while we discover ourselves in spiritual-physical communion with every being in the sacred commons. Thomas reminds us that spiritual energy emerges from the whole, from within the total complex of Earth functions.

Night prayer during Thursday's Dark hour gives us pause to consider *"The Great Work"* we have undertaken, and the horizon of its origins and purpose. Thomas prompts us to understand that our sense of who we are and what our role is must begin where the universe begins. Our work as planetary citizens is not simply to build the structures for a human world, but to become the media by which spirit might express its great work for the whole.

Humans cannot simply do as they please
with the natural world.
Humans likewise cannot do as they please
in relation to the psychic and spiritual forces
of the world,
but must enter into communion with these powers.

On Fridays when Thomas may have prayed the liturgical office with his Passionist brothers, the texts and themes were somber since that was the day of remembrance of the Passion of Christ, the passion of incarnate divinity. Mindful of that, this Berrian Breviary orients our Earth hours to face into the suffering of our planet. It is a day to consider *"Desolation and Destiny."* In unvarnished straight talk Thomas wants us to understand that the time has now come when we will listen to the living/dying Earth, or we will perish. Perhaps even more stunning is his charge that

When we destroy the living forms of this planet
we destroy modes of divine presence.

Traditionally, in the Christian form, Saturday is reserved for the veneration of Mary, honored as the Mother of divinity, the Mother of mysteries, the great Mother. It surprised me to discover how deep was Thomas's own devotion to the Madonna of Western faith, noted in the Passionist practice even to bear her name: Thomas Mary Berry. During the four prayer hours of this day we are drawn into rich Berrian poetics that celebrate the feminine dynamics and features of the cosmos under the banner: *Pax Gaia*. Thomas willed that we bring back the ancient symbol of the universe as the Great Mother, and whispers this prayer of promise to give us hope:

> *Our long motherless period may be coming to a close;*
> *hopefully, the long period of our mistreatment*
> *of planet Earth*
> *is being terminated.*

At last, we come round again to the great Sabbath, but now to celebrate not the original and forever "flaring forth" of existence, but to energetically anticipate the time that is to come: *"The Ecozoic."* This is the day that awakens us from a planetary nightmare to engender a new dream, a waking dream that we are called to quicken in the depths of our communal psychic generativity. It is the spiritual work of each of us and all of us together to dream the terrestrial paradise again.

> *In the beginning was the dream.*
> *Through the dream all things were made,*
> *and without the dream nothing was made*
> *that has been made.*
> *While all things share in this dream,*
> *as humans we share in this dream in a special manner.*

> *This is the entrancement,*
> *the magic of the world about us,*
> *its mystery, its ineffable quality.*

The generative, if not shamanic, practice of dreaming the new Earth has already begun. Indeed, we conjure this future hour by hour during the faithful days of our *Ecozoic* exercises. Such spiritual creativity is happening everywhere, all the time.

The *Ecozoic* is in gestation. Our great contemplative work is to be at once the fertile womb for its birthing and the midwives who aid in bringing it forth.

May all of us who present ourselves in the temple
of the Living Earth
at dawn, mid-day, dusk, and dark receive her reviving grace,
in communion with all beings, in the spirit of Thomas. Amen.

Kathleen Deignan, CND
June 1, 2024
Anniversary of the
Transition of Thomas Berry

Prologue

"The Meadow Across the Creek"

Thomas Berry

I was a young person then, some twelve years old. My family was moving from a more settled part of a Southern town out to the edge of town where the new house was still being built. The house, not yet finished, was situated on a slight incline. Down below was a small creek and there across the creek was a meadow. It was an early afternoon in May when I first looked down over the scene and saw the meadow. The field was covered with lilies rising above the thick grass. A magic moment, this experience gave to my life something, I know not what, that seems to explain my life at a more profound level than almost any other experience I can remember.

It was not only the lilies. It was the singing of the crickets and the woodlands in the distance and the clouds in an otherwise clear sky. It was not something conscious that happened just then. I went on about my life as any young person might do. Perhaps it was not simply this moment that made such a deep impression upon me. Perhaps it was a sensitivity that was developed throughout my childhood. Yet, as the years pass, this moment returns to me, and whenever I think about my basic life attitude and the whole trend of my mind and the causes that I have given my efforts to, I seem to come back to this moment and the impact it has had on my feeling for what is real and worthwhile in life.

This early experience, it seems, has become normative for me throughout the range of my thinking. Whatever preserves and enhances this meadow in the natural cycles of its transformation is good; what is opposed to this meadow or negates it is not good. My life orientation is that simple. It is also that pervasive. It applies in economics and political orientation as well as in education and religion and whatever.

That is good in economics that fosters the natural processes of this meadow. That is bad in economics that diminishes the capacity of this meadow to renew itself each spring and to provide a setting in which crickets can sing and birds can feed. As in economics so in jurisprudence and law and political affairs.

That is good which recognizes the rights of this meadow and the creek and the woodlands beyond to exist and flourish in their ever-renewing seasonal expression even while larger processes shape the bioregion in the larger sequence of transformations.

Religion too, it seems to me, takes its origin here in the deep mystery of this setting. The more a person thinks of the infinite number of interrelated activities taking place here, the more mysterious it all becomes, the more meaning a person finds in the Maytime blooming of the lilies, the more awestruck a person might *be in simply looking out over this little patch of meadowland. It had none of the majesty of the Appalachian or the Western mountains, none of the immensity or the power of oceans, nor even the harsh magnificence of desert country; yet in this little meadow the magnificence of life as celebration is manifested in a manner as profound and as impressive as any other place that I have known in these past many years.*

It seems to me we all had such experiences before we entered into an industrial way of life.

A New Story

Dawn

Enter into the grand liturgy of the universe.

INVOCATION

The epic of evolution.
The story of the universe.
This is our sacred story.
The ultimate mystery whence all things come into being.

DOXOLOGY

The universe is
the primary revelation of the divine,
the primary scripture,
the primary locus of divine-human communion.

Opening Verse

We need a story that will educate us,
a story that will heal, guide, and discipline us.

Hymn

Tell me a story.
Tell me the story of the river and the valley
and the streams and woodlands and wetlands,
of the shellfish and finfish.

Tell me a story.
A story of where we are and how we got here
and the characters and roles that we play.

Tell me a story,
a story that will be my story
as well as the story of everyone
and everything about me,

the story that brings us together
in a valley community,
a story that brings together the human community
with every living being in the valley,

a story that brings us together
under the arc of the great blue sky in the day
and the starry heavens at night,

a story that will drench us with rain
and dry us in the wind,

a story told by humans to one another
that will also be
the story that the wood thrush sings in the thicket,
the story that the river recites in its downward journey,
the story that Storm King Mountain
images forth in the fullness of its grandeur.

ANTIPHON

We bear the universe in our beings
as the universe bears us in its being.

PSALM

The story of the universe
is the story of the emergence of a galactic system
in which each new level of expression
emerges through the urgency of self-transcendence.

Hydrogen in the presence
of some millions of degrees of heat
emerges into helium.
After the stars take shape
as oceans of fire in the heavens,
they go through a sequence of transformations.
Some eventually explode into the stardust

out of which the solar system
and the Earth take shape.

Earth gives unique expression of itself
in its rock and crystalline structures
and in the variety and splendor of living forms,
until humans appear
as the moment in which the unfolding universe
becomes conscious of itself.

The human emerges
not only as an Earthling,
but also as a worldling.

We bear the universe in our beings
as the universe bears us in its being.

The two have a total presence to each other
and to that deeper mystery
out of which both the universe and ourselves
have emerged.

Psalm Prayer

The Earth is a single highly differentiated community. This is
the quintessential way of understanding the universe.

Reading

One of the more remarkable achievements of the twentieth century is our ability to tell the story of the Universe from empirical observation and with amazing insight into the sequence of transformations that has brought into being the Earth, the living world, and the human community. There seems, however, to be little realization of just what this story means in terms of the larger interpretation of the human venture.

For peoples, generally, their story of the universe and the human role in the universe is their primary source of intelligibility and value. Only through this story of how the universe came to be in the beginning and how it came to be as it is does a person come to appreciate the meaning of life or to derive the psychic energy needed to deal effectively with those crisis moments that occur in the life of the individual and in the life of the society. Such a story is the basis of ritual initiations throughout the world.

Versicle

Our story not only interprets the past; it also guides and inspires our shaping of the future. It communicates the most sacred mysteries.

~Silence~

We cannot understand any part of the universe until we understand how it functions in the whole.

CANTICLE

See the Earth in its sequence of transformations
as so many movements in a musical composition.

We now live not so much in a cosmos
as in a Cosmogenesis;
that is, a universe ever coming into being
through an irreversible sequence of transformations,
moving, in the larger arc of its development,
from a lesser to a greater order of complexity,
and from a lesser to great consciousness.

See the Earth in its sequence of transformations
as so many movements in a musical composition.

The sequence of events that emerges in time
needs to be understood simultaneously, as in music:
the earlier notes are gone
when the later notes are played,
but the musical phrase, indeed, the entire symphony,
needs to be heard simultaneously,
we do not fully understand the opening notes
until the later notes are heard.

See the Earth in its sequence of transformations
as so many movements in a musical composition.

Each new theme alters the meaning
of the early theme and the entire composition.
The theme resonates throughout
all the latter parts of the piece.

So too the origin moment of the universe
presents us with an amazing process
that we begin to appreciate
as a mystery unfolding through the ages.

INTERCESSIONS

EVOCATION

We are supported
by that same process
that brought the Earth into being,
that power that spun the galaxies into space,
that lit the sun and brought the moon into its orbit.

Those same forces are still present;
We feel their impact and understand
that we are not isolated in the chill of space
with the burden of the future upon us
and without the aid of any other power.

We are supported by that power
that spun the galaxies into space.

CLOSING PRAYER

The primordial emergence was the beginning of the Earth story, as well as the beginning of the personal story of each of us, since the story of the universe is the story of each individual being in the universe.

Day

*The universe constitutes
a single multiform sequential
celebratory event.*

INVOCATION

The natural world will once again
become a scriptural text—
the story written not in any verbal text
but in the very structure of the universe,
in the galaxies of the heavens
and in the forms of the Earth.

DOXOLOGY

The universe is
the primary revelation of the divine,

the primary scripture,
the primary locus of divine-human communion.

Exhortation

Become capable once again
of experiencing the immediacy of life,
the entrancing presence to the natural phenomena about us.
Return to the primordial community
of the universe, Earth, and all living beings.

Antiphon

Nothing can ever be separated from anything else.

Psalm

The New Story of the universe
is a biospiritual story
as well as a galactic story
and an Earth story.

The universe as we now know it
is integral with itself
throughout its vast extent in space
and throughout the long series
of its transformations in time.

Everywhere, at all times,
and in each of its particular manifestations,
the universe is present to itself.

Each atomic element
is immediately influencing and being influenced
by every other atom of the universe.

Nothing can ever be separated from anything else.

Psalm Prayer

It takes a universe to bring humans into being, a universe to educate humans, a universe to fulfill the human mode of being. More immediately, it takes a solar system and a planet Earth to shape, educate, and fulfill the human.

Meditation

The journey, the sacred journey of the universe, is the personal journey of each individual. The universe is the larger self of each person, since the entire sequence of events that has transpired since the beginning of the universe was required to establish each of us in the precise structure of our own being and in the larger context in which we function.

Reflection

PRAYER

The reality inherent in the original flaring forth could not be known until the shaping forces held in this process had brought forth the galaxies, the Earth, the multitude of living species, and the reflection of the universe on itself in human intelligence.

LESSON

From our vantage point we can sketch out the great story of the universe from its beginning until now. We can recognize the Earth as a privileged planet and see the whole as evolving out of some cosmic imaginative process. Any significant thought or speech about the universe finds its expression through such imaginative powers. Even our scientific terms have a highly mythic content—such words as energy, life, matter, form, universe, gravitation, evolution. Even such terms as atom, nucleus, electron, molecule, cell, organism. Each of these terms spills over into metaphor and mystery as soon as it is taken seriously.

We have substituted our real world of facts and figures for our visionary world. We must reflect, however, on what we have gained in this substitution and what we have lost. We have lost our principal means of entering into the primordial directive and sustaining forces of the universe. We have in a very special manner lost our presence to the life-sustaining forces of the Earth.

Whatever our gains in terms of scientific advances or in our industrial economy, neither of these is very helpful in establishing an integral presence to the more profound depths of our own being or into the more powerful forces shaping both the universe and the planet on which we live.

COLLECT

The natural world offers us wonder for the mind,
beauty for the imagination, and intimacy for the emotions.

EXAMEN

We must wonder at ourselves and what we are doing and what is happening to the larger destinies of the Earth.

We live too deeply alienated from the cosmological order, the phenomenal world, the world of the *"shining forth"* (for such is the meaning of the word *phenomena*).

Thus we need to know how to participate creatively in the wildness of the world about us. For it is out of the wild depths of the universe, and of our own being, that the greater visions must come.

CONFESSION

* We have contaminated the air, the water, the soil:
  Earth Have Mercy

* We have dammed the rivers, cut down the rainforests, destroyed animal habitat on an extensive scale:
  Cosmos Have Mercy

✳   We have driven the great blue whale and a multitude of
    animals almost to extinction:
    Earth Have Mercy

BENEDICTION

Live within the Covenant of the Universe, the ontological
covenant whereby each component of the universe experiences
itself in intimate rapport with the other components of the
universe.

Understand that we ourselves activate one of the deepest
dimensions of the universe.

Dusk

The universe that human intelligence knows
is the only universe
that could possibly produce human intelligence.

INVOCATION

Such a fantastic universe,
with its great spiraling galaxies, its supernovas,
our solar system, and this privileged planet Earth!
All held together in the vast curvature of space.

DOXOLOGY

The universe is
the primary revelation of the divine,

the primary scripture,
the primary locus of divine-human communion.

Opening Verse

The universe is the communion of each reality
of the universe with every other reality in the universe.
Here our scientific evidence confirms
the ancient awareness that we live in a *universe*—
a single, if multiform, energy event.

Hymn

Every particle of the universe tells the story
   in its own context.
The humans articulate this story in a particular human way,
the whales do it in their way, the birds do it in their way,
the worms in the earth do it in their way,
the insects do it in their way.

Every particle of the universe tells the story
   in its own context.
It's a kind of symphonic process.

Antiphon I

Participate in the intimacy of all things with each other.

Psalm I

Go beyond all the light and noise of the city
and look up at the sky overarching the Earth.

At this time in the evening,
we see the stars begin to appear
as the sun disappears over the horizon.

The light of day gives way
to the darkness of night.
A stillness, a healing quiet,
comes over the landscape.

It is a moment when some other world
makes itself known,
some numinous presence
beyond human understanding.

We experience the wonder of things
as the vast realms of space overwhelm
the limitations of our human minds.

At this moment, as the sky turns golden
and the clouds reflect the blazing colors of evening,
we participate in the intimacy of all things with each other.

Parents hold their children more closely
and tell stories to the children

as they go off into dreamland,
wonderful stories of times gone by,
stories of the animals,
of the good fairies,
adventure stories of heroic wanderings
through the wilderness,
stories of dragons threatening to devour the people,
and of courageous persons
who saved our world in perilous times.

These final thoughts of the day
are continued in the minds of children
as even in their sleep
they begin to dream of their own future,
dreams of the noble deeds
that would give meaning to their lives.
Whether awake or asleep,
the world of wonder fills their minds,
the world of beauty fills their imaginations,
the world of intimacy fills their emotions.

Antiphon II

The beginning of wisdom in any human activity is reverence.

Psalm II

The universe carries in itself
the norm of authenticity of every spiritual,
as well as every physical activity within it.

The spiritual and the physical
are dimensions of the single reality
that is the universe itself.

There is an ultimate wildness in all this,
for the universe, as existence itself,
is a terrifying as well as a benign mode of being.

If it grants amazing powers over much of this,
we must always remember that any arrogance on our part
will ultimately be called into account.

The beginning of wisdom in any human activity
is a certain reverence before the primordial mystery of
    existence,
for the world is a fearsome mode of being.

Psalm Prayer

Every being in the universe is intimately present to, and is
influencing, every other being in the universe.
    Every being contributes to the magnificence of the whole.

It's all a question of story. We are in trouble just now because we do not have a good story. We are in between stories. The old story, the account of how the world came to be and how we fit into it, is no longer effective. Yet we have not learned the new story. Our traditional story of the universe sustained us for a long period of time. It shaped our emotional attitudes, provided us with life purposes, and energized action. It consecrated suffering and integrated knowledge. We awoke in the morning and knew where we were. We could answer the questions of our children.

We could identify crime, punish transgressors. Everything was taken care of because the story was there. It did not necessarily make people good, nor did it take away the pains and stupidities of life or make for unfailing warmth in human association. It did provide a context in which life could function in a meaningful manner.

~SILENCE~

RESPONSORY

We understand the story of the universe as an emergent process with a fourfold sequence: the galactic story, the Earth story, the life story, and the human story. Together these constitute for us the primordial sacred story of the universe.

CANTICLE

The child awakens to a universe.
The mind of the child to a world of wonder.
Imagination to a world of beauty.
Emotions to a world of intimacy.

It takes a universe to make a child
both in outer form and inner spirit.
It takes a universe to educate a child,
a universe to fulfill a child.

Each generation presides
over the meeting of these two
in the succeeding generation.

So that the Universe is fulfilled in the child,
and the child is fulfilled in the Universe.
While the stars ring out in the heavens!

INTERCESSIONS

EVOCATION

We are supported by that same process
that brought the Earth into being,
that power that spun the galaxies into space,
that lit the sun and brought the moon into its orbit.

Those same forces are still present;
We feel their impact and understand
that we are not isolated in the chill of space
with the burden of the future upon us
and without the aid of any other power.
We are supported by that power
that spun the galaxies into space.

CLOSING PRAYER

The universe as a whole and in each of its individual components has an intangible inner form as well as a tangible physical structure. This deep form expressed in its physical manifestation entrances us—the fascination, the mystery, the immeasurable depths of the universe into which we are plunged with each of our experiences of the world about us.

Dark

*If the human has a psychic-spiritual mode
of being,
then the universe must be
a psychic-spirit-producing process.*

INVOCATION

The wonder and majesty of the universe
evokes the sense of the divine origin
and sacred character of the universe.
The universe is a mysterious reality.

DOXOLOGY

The universe is
the primary revelation of the divine,

the primary scripture,
the primary locus of divine-human communion.

Opening Verse

The dazzling course of things is exciting indeed.
The mysterious moment when the galactic formations took shape and the stars were formed throughout the heavens deserves celebration.

Hymn

Awareness of the all-pervading mysterious energy
articulated in the infinite variety of natural phenomena
seems to be the primordial experience of human
    consciousness,
awakening to an awesome universe filled with mysterious
    power.

Not only is energy our primary experience;
energy with its multiple modes of expression
is also the primary concern of modern physics,
its ultimate term of reference in describing
the most fundamental reality of the universe.

The universe can be seen as a single,
if multiform, energy event,

just as a particle such as a photon
is itself perceived as an energy event.

Antiphon

The universe is present to itself.

Psalm

The universe is an interacting community
throughout its full extent in space
and its development in time.

The universe is present to itself
in each of its innumerable modes of expression.

This is especially true with regard to the planet Earth.
The harm or benefit of any part
is experienced throughout the entire planet.

Psalm Prayer

Experience the universe with sensitivity and gratitude! These
are primary experiences of an awakening human consciousness. Such stupendous moments reveal a striking sense of the
alluring Earth.

~Silence~

Litany

Be listening

- ✳ to the stars in the heavens and the Sun and the moon,
- ✳ to the mountains and the plains,
- ✳ to the forests and rivers and seas that surround us,
- ✳ to the meadows and the flowering grasses,
- ✳ to the songbirds and the insects and
- ✳ to their music especially in the evening and the early hours of the night.

We need to experience, to feel, and to see these myriad creatures all caught up in the celebration of life.

Closing Prayer

Tonight as we look up at the evening sky, with the stars emerging against the fading background of the sunset, we think of the mythic foundations of our future. We need to engage in a shared dream experience.

The Mystery
of Meadow

Dawn

Experience the immediacy of life,
the entrancing presence
to the natural phenomena about us.

INVOCATION

We share our existence with the animals
and with all natural phenomena.
We form one body with heaven, Earth,
and all living things.

DOXOLOGY

These three commitments—
to the natural world as revelatory,

to the Earth community as our primary loyalty,
and to the progress of the community in its integrity.

Opening Verse

One of the finest moments
in our new sensitivity to the natural world
is our discovery of the Earth as a living organism.

Hymn

The wilderness world rediscovered
with heightened emotional sensitivity;

The world of life, of spontaneity,
the world of dawn and sunset
and glittering stars in the dark night heavens,

the world of wind and rain,
of meadow flowers and flowing streams,
of hickory and oak and maple
and spruce and pineland forests,

the world of desert sand and prairie grasses,
and within all this the eagle and the hawk,
the mockingbird and the chickadee,
the deer and the wolf and the bear,
the coyote, the raccoon, the whale and the seal,
and the salmon returning upstream to spawn—

All this, the wilderness world rediscovered
with heightened emotional sensitivity.

ANTIPHON

Every being has its own self, its mystery, its numinous aspect.

PSALM

Interior articulation of its own reality
is the immediate responsibility of every being.

Every being has its own interior,
its self, its mystery, its numinous aspect.
To deprive any being of this sacred quality
is to disrupt the larger order of the universe.
Reverence will be total or it will not be at all.

The universe does not come to us in pieces
any more than a human individual
stands before us with some part of its being.

Preservation of this feeling for reality in its depths
has been considerably upset in these past two centuries
of scientific analysis and technological manipulation
of the Earth and its energies.

During this period, the human mind
lived in the narrowest bonds
that it has ever experienced.

The vast mythic, visionary, symbolic world
with its all-pervasive numinous qualities was lost.

Because of this loss,
we made our terrifying assault upon the Earth
with an irrationality that is stunning in enormity,
while we were being assured
that this was the way to a better,
more humane, more reasonable world.

Psalm Prayer

Each individual being is supported by every other being in the community. In turn, each being contributes to the well-being of every other being in the community.

Reading

Throughout the Asian world terms designating supremely affectionate qualities carry ultimate cosmological significance. So, in the Chinese world, *jen,* a term translated as love, benevolence, or affection, is not only an emotional-moral term, it is also a cosmic force. This can be said also of the virtue of *ch'eng,* translated as sincerity or integrity. In India, the term *bhakti,* devotional love, was a cosmological as well as a spiritual force. In the Buddhist tradition, the term *karuna,* compassion, is a supreme cosmic power. Thus we find a pervasive intimacy and compassionate quality in the very structure of the universe and of the Earth itself.

Our own quest for a more intimate and benevolent human presence to the Earth and our times might reflect these precedents. But even more we might consider our intimate and compassionate presence to the Earth as originating ultimately in the curvature of space, as it is presented in modern science.

VERSICLE

Our inner spiritual world cannot be activated without experience of the outer world of wonder for the mind, beauty for the imagination, and intimacy for our emotions.

~SILENCE~

RESPONSORY

If we lived on the moon, our mind and emotions, our speech, our imagination, our sense of the divine would all reflect the desolation of the lunar landscape.

CANTICLE

If we have a wonderful sense of the divine,
it is because we live amid such awesome magnificence.

If we have refinement of emotion and sensitivity,
it is because of the delicacy, the fragrance,
and the indescribable beauty
of song and music and rhythmic movement
in the world about us.

If we have powers of imagination,
these are activated by the magic display
of color and sound, of form and movement,
such as we observe in the clouds of the sky,
the trees and bushes and flowers,
the waters and the wind,
the singing birds,
and the movement of the great blue whale
through the sea.

If we have words
with which to speak and think and commune,
words for the inner experience of the divine,
words for the intimacies of life,
if we have words to tell stories to our children,
words with which we can sing,
it is again because of the impressions we have received
from the variety of beings about us.

INTERCESSIONS

EVOCATION

We must feel that we are supported
by that same process that brought the Earth into being,
that power that spun the galaxies into space,
that lit the sun and brought the moon into its orbit.

Those same forces are still present;
indeed, we might feel their impact at this time and
    understand
that we are not isolated in the chill of space
with the burden of the future upon us
and without the aid of any other power.

We are supported by that power
that spun the galaxies into space.

Closing Prayer

If we grow in our life vigor, it is because the earthly community challenges us, forces us to struggle to survive, but in the end reveals itself as a benign providence. But however benign, it must provide that absorbing drama of existence whereby we can experience the thrill of being alive in a fascinating and unending sequence of adventures.

Day

A magic world! Enchanting.

INVOCATION

The vision of Earth-human development
will provide the sustaining dynamic
of the contemporary world.
Nourish awareness of this vision.

DOXOLOGY

These three commitments—
to the natural world as revelatory,
to the Earth community as our primary loyalty,
and to the progress of the community in its integrity.

Exhortation

Re-enchantment with the Earth as a living reality is the condition for our rescue of the Earth from the impending destruction that we are imposing upon it. To carry this out effectively, we must now, in a sense, reinvent the human as species within the community of life species. Our sense of reality and value must consciously shift from the anthropocentric to a biocentric norm of reference.

Antiphon

A pattern of life, a great liturgy, a celebration of existence.

Psalm

Dawn and sunset are moments
when the numinous source of all existence
is experienced with special sensitivity.

In springtime the flowering world
sets forth its blossoms.
The birds appear in the brilliance of their coloring,
in the ease and skill of their flight,
and in the beauty of their song.

Then there are the fearsome moments
when thunder rolls across the heavens

and the lightning shatters both
the sky and the Earth.

In the Northern Hemisphere
when autumn comes
the fruits appear, the birds depart,
the leaves fall, darkness settles over the land.

In the various tropical regions
the rains come more fully
in their seasonal sequence.

Living things come into being,
flourish, then fade from the scene.
This ever-renewing sequence of sunrise and sunset,
of seasonal succession, constitutes a pattern of life,
a great liturgy, a celebration of existence.

Psalm Prayer

Our fulfillment is not in our isolated human grandeur, but in
our intimacy with the larger Earth community, for this is the
larger dimension of our being. Our human destiny is integral
with the destiny of the Earth.

Meditation

Although intimacy exists with the stars in the heavens and with
the flowering forms of Earth, the presence of humans with the

other members of the natural world has a mutual responsiveness unknown to these other modes of being throughout the universe. That is unique, that can come to us from no other source. The animals can do for us, both physically and spiritually, what we cannot do for ourselves or for each other. These more precious gifts they provide through their presence and their responsiveness to our inner needs.

The term *anima* is the word used to identify a living or animated or ensouled being. While the word *soul* has been abandoned by scientists lest it compromise the empirical foundations of their study, the reality of the thought expressed remains forever embedded in the language that we use. The term *animal* will forever indicate an ensouled being.

PRAYER

A new sense of the Earth and its revelatory import is arising. The Earth will not be ignored, nor will it long endure being despised, neglected, or mistreated. The dynamics of creation are demanding attention once more.

LESSON

We do not judge the universe.
The universe is even now judging us.
This judgment, we experience as the "wild."
We recognize this presence
when we are alone in the forest,
especially in the dark of night,

or when we are at sea in a small craft
out of sight of land,
and for a moment lose our sense of direction.

The wild is experienced in the earthquakes
that shake the continents in such violence,
so too in the hurricanes that rise out of the sea
and sweep over the land.
We have at times thought
that we could domesticate the world,
for it sometimes appears as possible,
as in our capacity to evoke the vast energies
hidden in the nucleus of the tiny atom.

When we invade the deepest,
most mysterious dimension of matter,
nature throws at us most deadly forces,
wild forces that we cannot deal with,
forces that causes us to fear
lest we be rendering the planet a barren place
for the vast range of living beings.

The wild dimension of existence,
the reverence and fear associated with the wild—
here is where life and existence and art itself begin.

COLLECT

We are now in a period when we become capable once again of experiencing the intimacy of life, the entrancing presence to the natural phenomena about us.

EXAMEN

We must wonder at ourselves and what we are doing and what is happening to the larger destinies of the Earth.

Voices are there in the wind, in the unconscious depths of our minds. Voices not primarily to indict us for our cruelties, but to identify the distortions in our relations with the land and its inhabitants, and also to guide us toward a mutually enhancing human-Earth relationship in this beautiful valley.

CONFESSION

* The Earth community is a wilderness community that will not be bargained with:
  Earth Have Mercy

* Nor will it simply be studied or examined or made an object of any kind:
  Cosmos Have Mercy

* Nor will it be domesticated or trivialized as a setting or vacation indulgence, except under duress and by op-

pressions which it cannot escape:
Earth Have Mercy

BENEDICTION

Without the perfection of each part, something is lacking from the whole. Each particular being in the universe is needed by the entire universe. With this understanding of our profound kinship with all life, we can establish the basis for a flourishing Earth community.

Dusk

*Cosmology is the unifying context
and the ultimate referent
for all human understanding.*

INVOCATION

Such a fantastic universe,
with its great spiraling galaxies,
its supernovas,
our solar system,
and this privileged planet Earth!

DOXOLOGY

These three commitments—
to the natural world as revelatory,

to the Earth community as our primary loyalty,
and to the progress of the community in its integrity.

Dawn and evening liturgies
give expression to natural phenomena
in their numinous qualities.

Hymn

We are returning to our native place after a long absence,
meeting once again with our kin in the Earth community.

For too long we have been away somewhere,
entranced with our industrial world
of wires and wheels, concrete and steel,
and our unending highways,
where we race back and forth in continual frenzy.

The world of life, of spontaneity, the world of dawn and
   sunset
and glittering stars in the dark night heavens,
the world of wind and rain,
of meadow flowers and flowing streams,
of hickory and oak and maple and spruce and pineland
   forests,

the world of desert sand and prairie grasses,
and within all this the eagle and the hawk,

the mockingbird and the chickadee,
the deer and the wolf and the bear,
the coyote, the raccoon, the whale and the seal,
and the salmon returning upstream to spawn—

all this, the wilderness world recently rediscovered
with heightened emotional sensitivity,
is an experience not far from that of Dante meeting Beatrice
at the end of the *Purgatorio,*
where she descends amid a cloud of blossoms.

It was a long wait for Dante, so aware of his infidelities,
yet struck anew and inwardly "pierced," as when,
hardly out of his childhood, he had first seen Beatrice.
The "ancient flame" was lit again in the depths of his being.

In that meeting,
Dante is describing not only a personal experience,
but the experience of the entire human community
at the moment of reconciliation with the divine
after the long period of alienation
and human wandering away from the true center.

Something of this feeling of intimacy we now experience
as we recover our presence within the Earth community.

Antiphon I

The universe itself had a prior intimate rapport with the human.

Psalm I

The universe was the world of meaning in earlier times,
the basic referent in social order,
in economic survival, in the healing of illness.

In that wide ambience, the muses dwelled
whence came the inspiration
of poetry and art and music.

The drum, heartbeat of the universe itself,
established the rhythm of dance
whereby humans entered into
the very movement of the natural world.

The numinous dimension of the universe
impressed itself upon the mind
through the vastness of the heavens
and the power revealed in thunder and lightning,
as well as through springtime renewal
of life after the desolation of winter.

Then, too, the general helplessness of the human
before all the threats to survival
revealed the intimate dependence of the human
on the integral functioning of things.

That the human had such intimate rapport
with the surrounding universe was possible

only because the universe itself
had a prior intimate rapport with the human.

Antiphon II

Marvel at the millionfold sequence of living forms.

Psalm II

The excitement of life and the sustaining of psychic vigor
are evoked by our participation in this magnificent process.

Even before we give expression to any intellectual statement
about the natural world, we stand in awe at the stars
splashed in such prodigal display across the heavens,
at the Earth in its shaping of the seas and the continents,
at the great hydrological cycles that lift such vast quantities
of water up from the seas and rain them down over the land
to nourish the meadows and the forests
and to refresh the animals as the waters flow down
through the valleys and back again to the seas.

We marvel, too, at the millionfold sequence of living forms,
from the plankton in the sea and the bacteria in the soil
to the larger life-forms that swim through the oceans
and grow up from the soil and move over the land.

Psalm Prayer

The discovery of the universe as an evolutionary process
is a new sense of the universe as a revelatory experience.

Epistle

Now that this awareness of the epic dimension of the evolutionary process begins to be seriously considered, a new world of understanding begins to appear on the horizon. My first thought is that we not try to write theology at this moment. My thought is that we celebrate the glory of the universe that is there before us.

We need to establish rituals for celebrating these transformation moments that have enabled the universe and the planet Earth to develop over these past many years. This would involve celebrating the primordial moment of emergence of the universe, and other transformation moments, such as the supernova collapse of the first generation of stars whereby the elements needed for life and consciousness came into existence.

We should especially celebrate that star out of which our own solar system was born and the various life-forms of Earth became possible.

We need have no doubt of the appropriateness of our celebration of the sacred in this epic narrative. Here we join the great wisdom traditions of the past. In the Epic of Evolution, science becomes a path to wisdom.

~Silence~

What is fascinating about intimate associations with various living forms of the Earth is that we are establishing not only an acquaintance with the general life and emotions of various species, but also an intimate rapport, even an affective relationship, with individual animals within their wilderness context.

Canticle

Some 65 million years ago the Cenozoic era began,
the period when life as we know it took shape.

A wildly creative period of divine fantasy and extravagant play.

During the Cenozoic the life systems of Earth
brought forth their most entrancing beauty.

This was the period of flowers in their unnumbered variety
and in all their gorgeous colors and fantastic shapes.

A wildly creative period of divine fantasy and extravagant play.

This was the period of music, of winds through the trees,
the call of the mockingbird, the song of the whales in the sea;
this period saw the flight of the osprey,
the colorful patterns on the wings of the butterfly,
the fireflies in the evening.

A wildly creative period of divine fantasy and extravagant play.

INTERCESSIONS

EVOCATION

We are supported by that same process
that brought the Earth into being,
that power that spun the galaxies into space,
that lit the sun and brought the moon into its orbit.
Those same forces are still present;
We feel their impact and understand
that we are not isolated in the chill of space
with the burden of the future upon us
and without the aid of any other power.
We are supported by that power
that spun the galaxies into space.

CLOSING PRAYER

The entire Earth Community is infolded in the compassionate curve whereby the universe bends inwardly in a manner sufficiently closed to hold all things together and yet remain sufficiently open so that compassion does not confine, but fosters, the creative process.

Dark

We form one body with heaven, Earth, and all living things.

INVOCATION

Every component of the Earth community, both living and non-living, has three rights: the right to be, the right to habitat or a place to be, and the right to fulfill its role in the ever-renewing processes of the Earth community.

To reduce any mode of being simply to that of a commodity within the community of existence is a betrayal.

DOXOLOGY

These three commitments—
to the natural world as revelatory,

to the Earth community as our primary loyalty,
and to the progress of the community in its integrity.

Opening Verse

This universe itself, but especially the planet Earth, needs to be experienced as the primary mode of divine presence, just as it is the primary educator, primary healer, primary commercial establishment, and primary lawgiver for all that exists within this life community.

Hymn

As Earth is a magic planet in the exquisite presence
of its diverse members to one another,
so this movement into the future must in some manner
be brought about in ways that are ineffable to the human
    mind.

Think of a viable future for the planet
less as the result of some scientific insight
or as dependent on some socioeconomic arrangement
than as participation in a symphony
or as renewed presence to some numinous presence
manifested in the wonderworld about us
vaguely experienced in that view of the lilies
blooming in the meadow across the creek.

Antiphon

The emergent universe is a revelatory experience.

Psalm

The emergent universe
is a revelatory experience
of numinous presence.

The simplest atomic structure,
the hydrogen atom,
already expresses a radiant intelligibility,
a psychic as well as a physical aspect of reality:
It is a numinous and mystical being
as well as a physical measurable being.
As the articulation of an energy quantum,
the primordial particles carry within themselves
the total mystery and meaning of the universe,
as well as the entire range of creativity that will ever exist.

Psalm Prayer

Our dreams of a more viable mode of being for ourselves and
for the planet Earth can only be distant expressions of the primordial source of the universe itself in its full extent in space
and in the long sequence of its transformations in time.

~Silence~

LITANY

The Earth is itself the
* primary physician,
* primary lawgiver,
* primary revelation of the divine,
* primary scientist,
* primary technologist,
* primary commercial venture,
* primary artist,
* primary educator,
* and primary agent in whichever other activity we find in human affairs.

CLOSING PRAYER

Now night has advanced.
The stars are more brilliant than ever.
The time has come for us to enjoy our final moments
with each other as we continue on our journey.

Tuesday

The Human Venture

Dawn

We must reinvent the human as species
within the community of life species.

INVOCATION

We might begin with some awareness of what it is to be human,
the role of consciousness on Earth, and the place of the human
species in the universe.

DOXOLOGY

The Universe,
the Earth,
and the Human
are centered in one another.

Opening Verse

In its human mode,
the universe reflects on and celebrates itself
in a unique mode of conscious self-awareness.

Hymn

Humans, in an earlier period
experienced themselves as owning nothing,
as receiving existence itself and life and consciousness
as an unmerited gift from the universe,
as having exuberant delight and unending gratitude
as their first obligation.

It was a personal universe,
a world of intimacy and beauty.

A universe where every mode of being
lived by a shared existence
with all other modes of being.

No being had meaning or reality or fulfillment
apart from the great community of life.

Antiphon

Continuing enhancement of life must be shared by all the
living.

Psalm

If there is to be real and sustainable progress,
it must be a continuing enhancement of life
for the entire planetary community.

It must be shared by all the living,
from the plankton in the sea
to the birds above the land.

It must include the grasses, the trees,
and the living creatures of the Earth.
True progress must sustain the purity
and life-giving qualities
of both the air and the water.

The integrity of these life systems
must be normative for any progress worthy of the name.
This is the order of magnitude of the task
that is before us.

Psalm Prayer

The human is a participatory reality.
We are members of the great universe community.
We are not on the outside looking in;
we are within the universe, awakening to the universe.
We participate in its life.

Reading

The change that is taking place on the Earth and in our minds is one of the greatest changes ever to take place in human affairs, perhaps *the* greatest, since what we are talking about is not simply another historical change or cultural modification, but a change of geological and biological as well as physiological order of magnitude. We are changing the Earth on a scale comparable only to the changes in the structure of the Earth and of life that took place during some hundreds of millions of years of Earth development.

Versicle

A vast mystery is being enacted
in which we participate in a unique fashion.

~Silence~

Responsory

The human is a mode of being of the universe
as well as a distinctive being in the universe.

Canticle

We bear within us the impress of every transformation
through which the universe and the planet Earth have
passed.

The elements out of which Earth and all its living beings
are composed were shaped by supernovae.

We passed through the period of stardust dispersion
resulting from this implosion-explosion
of a first-generation star.

We were integral with the attractive forces
that brought those particles together
in the original shaping of Earth.

We felt the gathering of the components
of the earthly community
and experienced the self-organizing spontaneities
within the megamolecules,
out of which came the earliest manifestations
of the life process and the transition
to cellular and organic living forms.

These same forces that brought forth the genetic codings
of all the various species were guiding the movement of life
toward its expression in human consciousness.

This journey, the sacred journey of the universe,
is the personal journey of each individual.
We cannot but marvel at this amazing sequence
of transformations.

Intercessions

Evocation

We are supported
by that same process
that brought the Earth into being,
that power that spun the galaxies into space,
that lit the sun and brought the moon into its orbit.
Those same forces are still present;
We feel their impact and understand
that we are not isolated in the chill of space
with the burden of the future upon us
and without the aid of any other power.
We are supported by that power
that spun the galaxies into space.

Closing Prayer

The human project has entered a period of heightened perils; it has also entered a period of new possibilities. All the creatures of Earth are looking to us for their destiny. Among these are our children and grandchildren, who depend on our decisions for the sustenance and flourishing of the life systems of the planet.

Day

*We have only begun to realize that we are,
precisely in our human mode of being,
a single if also an immensely significant
component in the great community of existence.*

INVOCATION

Awaken in us an awareness of the need we have for all the living companions that we have with us here on our homeland planet. To lose any of these splendid companions is to diminish our own lives.

DOXOLOGY

The Universe,
the Earth,

and the Human
are centered in one another.

EXHORTATION

The natural world will once again become a scriptural text.

The story is written not in any verbal text but in the very structure of the universe, in the galaxies of the heavens and in the forms of the Earth. These are phases in the great story that is the primary presentation whereby the ultimate mystery of things reveals itself to us. The sacred community will be recognized as including the entire universe. One thing we may be sure of: the human community and the natural world will go into the future as a single sacred community or we will both experience disaster.

ANTIPHON

We are just emerging from a technological entrancement.

PSALM

We have before us the question
not simply of physical survival,
but of survival in a human mode of being,

survival and development into intelligent,
affectionate, imaginative persons
thoroughly enjoying the universe about us,

living in profound communion with one another
and with some significant capacities to express ourselves
in our literature and creative arts.

We are just emerging from a technological entrancement.

It is a question of interior richness
within our own personalities,
of shared understanding with others,
and of a concern that reaches out
to all the living and nonliving beings of the Earth,
and in some manner out to the distant stars in the heavens.

Psalm Prayer

Our relationship with Earth involves something more than pragmatic use, academic understanding, or aesthetic appreciation. A truly human intimacy with Earth and with the entire natural world is needed.

Meditation

The Earth that directed itself instinctively in its former phases seems now to be entering a phase of conscious decision through its human expression. This is the ultimate daring venture for the Earth, this confiding its destiny to human decision, the bestowal upon the human community of the power of life and death over its basic life systems. Something strange indeed is happening to the entire process, and we must wonder at ourselves and what we are doing and what is happening to the larger destinies of the Earth, even perhaps of the universe.

REFLECTION

PRAYER

Alienation is overcome as soon as we experience this surge of energy from the source that has brought the universe through the centuries. New fields of energy become available to support the human venture. These new energies find expression and support in celebration.

LESSON

One of the significant historical roles of the primal people of the world is not simply to sustain their own traditions, but to call the entire civilized world back to a more authentic mode of being.

Our only hope is in a renewal of those primordial experiences out of which the shaping of our more sublime human qualities could take place.

While our own experiences can never again have the same immediacy or the compelling quality that characterized this early period, we are experiencing a post-critical naïveté, a type of presence to the Earth and all its inhabitants that includes, and also transcends, the scientific understanding that now is available to us from these long years of observation and reflection.

Native peoples in their long traditional mystique of the Earth, are emerging as one of the surest guides into a viable future.

COLLECT

In the realm of consciousness, a supreme mode of communion exists within the individual, with the human community, within the Earth-human complex. Increased capacity for personal identity is inseparable from this capacity for mutual presence. It is the mission of our present and all future generations to develop this capacity for mutual presence on new and more comprehensive levels.

EXAMEN

We must wonder at ourselves and what we are doing and what is happening to the larger destinies of the Earth.

To be educated is to know the story and the human role in the story. Through this story we come to know the manner whereby we ourselves came into being and the role we should be fulfilling in the story.

CONFESSION

✳ All human processes, undisciplined expansion and self-inflation lead only to destruction:
  Earth Have Mercy

* Apart from the well-being of Earth, no subordinate life system can survive:
  Cosmos Have Mercy

* Any particular activity must find its place within the larger pattern, or it will die and perhaps bring down the larger life system itself:
  Earth Have Mercy

BENEDICTION

We have begun to realize that the Earth is an awesome mystery, ultimately as fragile as we ourselves are fragile. But our responsibility to the Earth is not simply to preserve it, it is to be present to the Earth in its next sequence of transformations.

While we were unknowingly carried through the evolutionary process in former centuries, the time has come when we must in some sense guide and energize the process ourselves.

To succeed in this task of shaping the future, the will of the more comprehensive self must be functioning. The individual will can function in this capacity only through an acknowledged union with the deeper structures of reality.

Even beyond union with the human community must be union with the Earth, with the universe itself in the full wonder of its being.

Dusk

*A new historical vision is emerging
to guide us on our way to a more creative
future.*

INVOCATION

What is needed is the deeper meaning of the relationship between the human community and the Earth process.

DOXOLOGY

The Universe,
the Earth,
and the Human
are centered in one another.

OPENING VERSE

The universe is the only self-referent mode of being in the phenomenal world. Every other being is universe-referent in itself and in its every activity.

HYMN

Air and water and soil and seeds
provide our basic sustenance,
sunshine that pours its energies over the landscape—
these are integral with the functioning of the fruitful Earth.

Physically and spiritually we are woven
into this living process.
As long as the integrity of the process is preserved,
we have air to breathe and water to drink
and nourishing food to eat.

ANTIPHON I

Mysterious forces guide earthly events.

PSALM I

We must simply respond to the urgencies
imposed on us by the energy
that holds the stars within the galactic clusters,
that shaped the planet under our feet,

that has guided life
through its bewildering variety of expression,
and that has found even higher expression
in the exotic tribes and nations,
languages, literature, art, music,
social forms, religious rituals,
and spiritual disciplines
over the surface of the planet.

There is reason to believe
that those mysterious forces
that have guided earthly events thus far
have not suddenly collapsed
under the great volume of human affairs.

What is clear is that the Earth
is mandating that the human community
assume a responsibility
never assigned to any previous generation.

ANTIPHON II

All became possible. We ourselves became possible.

PSALM II: PSALM OF THE CELL

For the more evolved multicellular
organic forms of life to appear
there had to appear the first living cell:

a procaryotic cell
capable, by the energy of the sun,
the carbon of the atmosphere,
and the hydrogen of the sea,
of a metabolic process never known previously.

This original moment of transition
from the nonliving to the living world,
was fostered by the fierce lightning
of these early times.

Then, at a critical moment
in the evolution of the original cell,
another cell capable of using
the oxygen of the atmosphere
with its immense energies appeared.

Photosynthesis was completed by respiration.

At this moment
the living world as we know it
began to flourish until it shaped the Earth anew.

Daisies in the meadows,
the song of the mockingbird,
the graceful movement of dolphins through the sea,
all these became possible at this moment.

We ourselves became possible.

New modes of music, poetry, and painting,
all these came into being in new forms
against the background
of the music and poetry and painting
of the celestial forms circling through the heavens.

Psalm Prayer

We can recognize in ourselves our special intellectual, emotional, and imaginative capacities.

That these capacities have existed as dimensions of the
universe from its beginning is clear since the universe is ever
integral with itself in all of its manifestations throughout its
vast extension in space and throughout the sequence of transformations in time.

Epistle

The ideal of a human habitat within a natural setting
of trees and fields and flowering plants,
of flowing streams and sea coasts
and those living forms that swim through the waters
and move over the land
and fly through the air—

a world of non-toxic rain and non-contaminated wells,
of unpolluted sea coast with its fertile wetlands—

the ideal of a human community integral with such a setting,
with all the severity of its demands on its human occupants,
would seem to be our only effective way
into a sustainable and humanly satisfying future.

~SILENCE~

RESPONSORY

We begin to appreciate the integral majesty of the natural
world, the need that every form of life has for every other form,
and the involvement of the human in the total process.

CANTICLE

This primordial Earth community itself
existed through the presence of the indwelling spirit
whence came its sacred character.

Whatever humans needed
was supplied by the surrounding world,
whatever inspiration for their imagination,
whatever awakening of intelligence,
whatever personal fulfillment.

This joyful fulfillment found expression
in poetry and music and song and dance,
a fulfillment that continues to find expression
in our children running through the meadows,

wading in the creeks, playing with animals,
or simply sitting with utmost satisfaction
in a backyard puddle experiencing the cooling delight
of such an environment on a summer's day.

Such is the beginning of education,
of aesthetic experience, of physical vigor,
of acquaintance with the universe.

This is the awakening of both the senses and the mind.
Ultimately it is the awakening of the universe to itself.

This is the beginning of poetry and music and literature.
It is the beginning of cosmology, of philosophical reflection,
of moral perception, of theological insight.

It is the beginning of the Epic of Evolution.

INTERCESSIONS

EVOCATION

We must feel that we are supported
by that same process that brought the Earth into being,
that power that spun the galaxies into space,
that lit the sun and brought the moon into its orbit.
Those same forces are still present;
indeed, we might feel their impact at this time
and understand that we are not isolated in the chill of space

with the burden of the future upon us
and without the aid of any other power.
We are supported by that power
that spun the galaxies into space.

CLOSING PRAYER

From the moment of awakening of our consciousness,
the universe strikes wonder and fulfillment
throughout our human mode of being.
Humans and the universe were made for each other.

Dark

*A degraded habitat
will produce degraded humans.*

INVOCATION

The most difficult transition to make is from an anthropo-centric to a biocentric norm of progress. If there is to be any progress, then the entire life community must progress.

DOXOLOGY

The Universe,
the Earth,
and the Human
are centered in one another.

Opening Verse

Any progress of the human at the expense of the larger life
community must ultimately lead to a diminishment of human
life itself.

Hymn

Until the human is understood
as a dimension of the Earth,
we have no secure basis for understanding
any aspect of the human.
We can understand the human only through the Earth.

Beyond the Earth, of course,
is the universe and the curvature of space.
This curve is reflected in the curvature of the Earth
and finally in that psychic curve
whereby the entire universe reflects back on itself
in human intelligence.

Thus the curve is sufficiently closed
to hold all things together
while it is sufficiently open
to continue its creative emergence into the future.

Antiphon

There is no Earth without the human.

Psalm

The remarkable world of human consciousness:
the thoughts and emotions,
the social forms and rituals of the human community,
are as much "Earth"
as are the soil and the rocks and the trees and the flowers.

We can reduce the flowers to the atoms
or the atoms to the flowers.

There are no atoms that are just atoms,
no flowers that are just flowers.

There is no Earth without the human;
no human without the Earth.
Any other Earth or any other human is a pure abstraction.

Psalm Prayer

The binding curve that draws all things together simultaneously produces with the inner forces of matter that expansive tension whereby the universe and the Earth continue on their creative course.

~Silence~

Litany

* What is needed is a bonding of all the various forms of life on the planet Earth into a single, yet differentiated, community.
* Even beyond the living forms, there is the urgency to establish a comprehensive community of all the constituents of the planet, both the geological and biological components.
* Even beyond this, there is the necessity for humans to recognize the unity of the universe itself.

There is ultimately only a single community.

Closing Prayer

To learn how to live graciously together
would make us worthy
of this unique, beautiful, blue planet
that evolved in its present splendor over some billions of
    years,
a planet that we should give over to our children
with the assurance
that this great community of the living
will lavish upon them
the care that it has bestowed so abundantly
upon ourselves.

Wednesday

A Communion
of Subjects

Dawn

*Subjectivity is the numinous quality
associated with every reality of the universe.*

INVOCATION

Every part of the universe
activates a particular dimension
or aspect of the universe
in a unique and unrepeatable manner.
Thus everything is needed.

DOXOLOGY

The Universe—
a vast multiplicity of individual realities

with both qualitative and quantitative differences
all in spiritual-physical communion with each other.

Opening Verse

"Friendship relation" exists among all things throughout the universe. Indeed, we cannot be truly ourselves in any adequate manner without all our companion beings throughout the Earth.

Hymn

Every being exists
in intimate relation with other beings
and in a constant exchange of gifts with each other.

But this relationship
is something beyond pragmatic use.
It is rather a mutual sharing of existence
in the grand venture of the universe itself.

Perceive the universe
as a single gorgeous celebration,
a cosmic liturgy that humans enter
through their ritual dances
at those moments of daily and seasonal change,
at dawn and sunset,
and at the equinox and solstice moments.

ANTIPHON

As we recover our awareness
of the universe as a communion of subjects,
a new interior experience awakens within the human.

PSALM

The thousandfold voices of the natural world
became inaudible to many humans.
The mountains, rivers, wind, and sea
all became mute insofar as humans were concerned.

The forests were no longer the abode
of an infinite number of spirit presences
but were simply so many broad feet of timber
to be "harvested" as objects used for human benefit.

Animals were no longer
the companions of humans
within the single community of existence.
They were denied not only their inherent dignity
but even their right to habitat.

As we recover our awareness
of the universe as a communion of subjects,
a new interior experience awakens within the human.
The barriers disappear.

An enlargement of soul takes place.
The excitement evoked by natural phenomena is renewed.

Dawn and sunset are once again
transforming experiences,
as are the sights, sounds, scents, tastes,
and feel of the natural world about us—
the surging sea,
the sound of the wind,
the brooding forests.

All this could be continued
in a never-ending list of experiences
that have been lost to large segments
of the human community in recent centuries—
not because the phenomena do not surround us constantly,
but because we have become locked into ourselves,
as though large segments of the human mind
have become paralyzed.

It is no wonder that humans
have devastated the planet so extensively.
It was only a collection of objects to be used.

PSALM PRAYER

Our intimacy with the universe demands presence to the
smallest particles, as well as to the vast range of stars splashed

across the skies in every direction—the grasses, the flowers, the forests, and the fauna that present themselves to our opening senses.

READING

This is the first value. The universe emerges as a differentiation process. Without differentiation there is no universe, there is no existent reality. From the beginning, after its brief period of almost formless radiation, the universe articulated itself in unique, identifiable, intelligible energy constellations, or patterns. Reality is not some infinitely extended homogeneous smudge. Each articulation is unrepeatable and irreplaceable at whatever level, from the subatomic to the galactic, from the iron core of the Earth to the flower, from the eagle in flight to the human persons who walk over the land. Each of these is a unique expression of the total Earth presence. At the human level the individual becomes almost a species, the unique quality of the individual becomes such a commanding presence.

The second value is subjectivity. Not only is the articulation of the individual reality so absolute in reference to otherness, this identity carries with it an interior depth, a special quality, a mystery that expresses not only a phenomenal mode, but also an archetypal realization. This enables each articulation of the real to resonate with that numinous mystery that pervades all the world. This quality of things is universal, but its activation in the human order provides the creative dynamics of the thinker, the poet, the writer, the scientist, the farmer, the craftsman, the political leader, the trader, the educator, and whichever other role is fulfilled by human beings in the functioning of the universe.

A third basis of value is communion, for every reality of the universe is intimately present to every other reality of the universe and finds its fulfillment in this mutual presence. The entire evolutionary process depends on communion. Without this fulfillment that each being finds in beings outside itself, nothing would ever happen in the entire world. There would be no elements, no molecules, no life, no consciousness.

VERSICLE

The interrelatedness of the universe in its every manifestation is what establishes the unity of the entire world and enables it to be a "universe."

~SILENCE~

RESPONSORY

Everywhere intimacy, the mutual presence of the life community in all its numinous qualities.

CANTICLE

The sacred is that which evokes wonder.
We know some things but only the shadow of things.
We go to the sea at night and stand along the shore.

We listen to the urgent roll of the waves
reaching ever higher until it reaches its limits and can go no
    farther,
then returns to its inward peace until the moon calls again
for its presence on these southern shores.
The lights of some distant city
keep us from that all-encompassing serenity
we long for but seldom attain.

INTERCESSIONS

EVOCATION

We must feel that we are supported
by that same power that brought the Earth into being,
that power that spun the galaxies into space,
that lit the sun and brought the moon into its orbit.
Those same forces are still present;
indeed, we might feel their impact at this time
and understand that we are not isolated
in the chill of space with the burden of the future upon us
and without the aid of any other power.

CLOSING PRAYER

Awaken in us an awareness of our need for all the living companions we have here on our homeland planet. To lose any of
these splendid companions is to diminish our own lives.

Day

The universe is a communion of subjects,
not a collection of objects—subjects
to be communed with as a divine manifestation.

INVOCATION

The universe in its emergence is neither determined nor random, but creative.

DOXOLOGY

The Universe—
a vast multiplicity of individual realities
with both qualitative and quantitative differences
all in spiritual-physical communion with each other.

Exhortation

A truly human intimacy with the Earth
and with the entire natural world is needed.
Our children should be properly introduced
to the world in which they live,
to the trees and grasses and flowers,
to the birds and the insects
and the various animals that roam over the land,
to the entire range of natural phenomena.

Antiphon

A spiritual bond between ourselves
and the natural world is needed.

Psalm

A treaty, or some spiritual bond,
between ourselves and the natural world, is needed,
a bonding based on the principle of mutual enhancement.

The river and its valley
are neither our enemy to be conquered,
nor our servant to be controlled,
nor our mistress to be seduced.

The river is a pervasive presence beyond all these.
It is the ultimate psychic context
as well as the physical context
out of which we emerge into being
and by which we are nourished, guided, healed, and fulfilled.

As the gulls soaring above the river in its estuary region,
as the blossoms along its banks,
the fish within its waters,
so, too, the river is a celebration of existence,
of life lived in intimate association
with the sky, the winds from every direction, the sunlight.

The river is the binding presence
throughout the valley community.

Psalm Prayer

The universe is a unity, an interacting and genetically related community of beings bound together in an inseparable relationship in space and time. The unity of planet Earth is especially clear; each being of the planet is profoundly implicated in the existence and functioning of every other being of the planet.

Meditation

To understand the human role in the functioning of Earth we need to appreciate the spontaneity found in every form of existence in the natural world, spontaneity that we associate with the wild—that which is uncontrolled by human dominance.

We have misconceived our role if we consider that our historical mission is to "civilize" or to "domesticate" the planet, as if the wilderness is something destructive rather than the ultimate, creative modality of any form of earthly being. We are not here to control. We are here to become integral with the larger Earth community. The community itself, and each of its members, has ultimately a wild component, a creative spontaneity that is its deepest reality, its most profound mystery.

We might reflect on this sense of the wild and the civilized when the dawn appears through the morning mist. At such time a stillness pervades the world—a brooding sense, a quiet transition from night into day. This experience deepens when evening responds to morning as day fades away, and night comes in the depth of its mystery.

We are most aware at such moments of transition that the world about us is beyond human control. So in the transition phases of human life: at birth, maturity, and death we brood over our presence in a world of mystery far greater than ourselves.

Prayer

Our knowledge of God comes to us from our acquaintance with the Earth, for the divine reveals itself first in the sky and in the waters, in the mountains and the valleys, in the birds of the air and in all those living forms that flower and move over the surface of the planet. By bringing forth the planet Earth in its living forms, and its human intelligence, the universe has found its most elaborate expression and manifestation of its deepest mystery.

Lesson

Every being has rights to be recognized and revered.
Trees have tree rights, insects have insect rights,
rivers have river rights, mountains have mountain rights.

So too with the entire range of beings
    throughout the universe.
All rights are limited and relative.
So too with humans. We have human rights.
We have rights to the nourishment and shelter we need.
We have rights to habitat.
But we have no rights to deprive other species
    of their proper habitat.
We have no rights to interfere with their migration routes.
We have no rights to disturb the basic functioning
of the biosystems of the planet.

Collect

We cannot own the Earth or any part of the Earth in any absolute manner. We own property in accord with the well-being of the property and for the benefit of the larger community as well as ourselves.

Examen

We must wonder at ourselves and what we are doing and what is happening to the larger destinies of the Earth.

Now, after these centuries of experiencing the planet as being a collection of objects for scientific analysis and commercial use, we must ask: Where can we find the resources for a reevaluation of our activities?

Confession

✳ If the Earth grows inhospitable toward human presence, it is primarily because we have lost our sense of courtesy toward the Earth and its inhabitants:
Earth Have Mercy

✳ If the Earth grows inhospitable toward human presence, it is because we have lost our sense of gratitude, our willingness to recognize the sacred character of habitat:
Cosmos Have Mercy

✳ If the Earth grows inhospitable toward human presence, it is because we have lost our capacity for the awesome, for the numinous quality of every earthly reality:
Earth Have Mercy

BENEDICTION

Our sense of the Earth must be sufficiently sound so that it can support the dangerous future that is calling us. It is a decisive moment. Yet we should not feel that we alone are determining the future course of events. The future shaping of the community depends on the entire Earth in the unity of its organic functioning, on its geological and biological as well as the human members.

Dusk

Move beyond democracy to biocracy,
to participation in the larger life community.

Invocation

Each form of life is integrated with every other life form.
Even beyond the Earth, by force of gravitation,
every particle of the physical world attracts
and is attracted to every other particle.
This attraction holds the differentiated universe together
and enables it to be a universe of individual realities.

Doxology

The Universe—
a vast multiplicity of individual realities

with both qualitative and quantitative differences
all in spiritual-physical communion with each other.

Opening Verse

Spiritual energy emerges in the total complex of Earth functions.

Hymn

Appreciate the dazzling wonder of
the sacred dimension
that finds expression
in the universe itself,
a universe that emerged into being
by a creativity beyond anything we can imagine,
a world that assumed its present form
by an unpredictable self-organizing power.

What is truly amazing is that these unpredictable processes,
sometimes considered to be random,
produced a universe so coherent in its structure
and so finely ordered in its functioning
amid the turbulence of an awesome
and relentless inner creative energy.

Antiphon I

We are finally awakening.

Psalm I

We are finally awakening to the beauty of this land.
We are finally accepting the discipline of this land.
We are finally listening to the teaching of this land.
We are finally absorbed in the delight of this land.

Today we begin to relieve an ancient wrong.
We wish especially to restore to this continent its ancient joy.
For while much of what we have done is beyond healing,
there is a resilience throughout the land that only
awaits its opportunity to flourish once again
with something of its ancient splendor.

Antiphon II

A new intimacy with the universe has begun.

Psalm II

A new intimacy with the universe has begun
within the context of our scientific tradition.

From the tiniest fragment of matter
to the grand sweep of the galactic systems,
we have a new clarity
through our empirical modes of knowing.

We are intimate with every particle of the universe
and with the vast design of the whole.
We see it and hear it and commune with it as never before.

Psalm Prayer

A way is opening to receive the spiritual heritage of the
   universe.
Central to this process is our contact with the sacred
and the vast range of Earth's psychic dynamism.

Epistle

Be mindful of the Earth, the planet out of which we are born
and by which we are nourished, guided, healed—the planet,
however, which we have abused to a considerable degree in
these past two centuries of industrial exploitation. The exploitation has reached such extremes that presently it appears that
some hundreds of thousands of species will be extinguished
before the end of the century.

~Silence~

Responsory

Even beyond union with the human community must be
union with the Earth, with the universe itself in the full wonder
of its being.

Only the Earth can adequately will the Earth. If we will the future effectively, it will be because the guidance and the powers of the Earth have been communicated to us, not because we have determined the future of the Earth simply with some rational faculty.

Our sense of the sacred can be recovered in the mystique of the Earth, in the epic of evolution. Spiritual disciplines are once again being renewed throughout the world.

CANTICLE

We are a pervasive presence.
We are that reality
in whom the entire Earth
comes to a special mode of reflexive consciousness.

We are ourselves
a mystical quality of the Earth itself,
a unifying principle,
an integration of the various polarities
of the material and the spiritual,
the physical and the psychic,
the natural and the artistic,
the intuitive and the scientific.

We are the unity
in which all these inhere
and achieve a special mode of functioning.

In this way the human acts as a pervading logos.

If the human is microcosmos,
the cosmos is macroanthropos.
We are each the cosmic person,
the *Mahapurusha*, the Great Person of Hindu India,
expressed in the universe itself.
This being so, there is need
to be sensitive to the Earth,
for the destiny of the Earth
identifies with our own destiny,
exploitation of the Earth
is exploitation of the human,
elimination of the aesthetic splendors of the Earth
is diminishment of existence.

We do not serve the human
by blasting the mountains apart
for mineral resources,
for in losing the wonder and awesome qualities of the
    mountains
we destroy an urgent dimension of our own reality.

INTERCESSIONS

EVOCATION

We must feel that we are supported
by that same process

that brought the Earth into being,
that power that spun the galaxies into space,
that lit the sun and brought the moon into its orbit.

Those same forces are still present;
indeed, we might feel their impact at this time
and understand that we are not isolated in the chill of space
with the burden of the future upon us
and without the aid of any other power.
We are supported by that power
that spun the galaxies into space.

CLOSING PRAYER

The natural world has produced its present variety, its abundance, and the creative interaction of all its components through billions of experiments. To shatter all this in the belief that we can gain by thwarting nature in its basic spontaneities is a brash and foolish thing. If we do not alter our attitude and our activities, our children and grandchildren will live not only amid the ruins of the industrial world, but also amid the ruins of the natural world itself. That this will not happen, is the hope that is before us.

Dark

*Listen to the various creatures of the Earth,
each telling its own story.*

Invocation

A way is opening for each person to receive the total spiritual heritage of the human community as well as the total spiritual heritage of the universe.

Doxology

The Universe—
a vast multiplicity of individual realities
with both qualitative and quantitative differences
all in spiritual-physical communion with each other.

Opening Verse

For some the ultimate mystery of things
is experienced in the depth of the inner self,
for others in the human community,
for still others in the Earth process itself.
Yet in each instance the full sense of communion
seems to be present.

Hymn

Advance the cause of peace
simply by being with each other.
Learn to trust and admire each other
and to share the traditions we represent.

Continue this presence to each other
by looking beyond ourselves
to the larger universe we live in.
Participate in the forgiveness, the peace,
the intimacy of all things with each other.

Discover the great community of the Earth,
a comprehensive community of all the living
and nonliving components of the planet.

Our intimacy with the Earth
is our way to intimacy with each other.

Antiphon

Nothing is completely itself without everything else.

Psalm

In virtue of relatedness,
everything is intimately present
to everything else in the universe.

Nothing is completely itself without everything else.

This relatedness is both spatial and temporal.
However distant in space or time,
the bond of unity is functionally there.

The universe is a communion and a community.
We ourselves are that communion
become conscious of itself.

Psalm Prayer

The discovery of human intimacy with all those other modes of
being that live with us on this planet, inspire our art and literature, reveal that numinous world whence all things come into
being, and with which we exchange the very substance of life.

~Silence~

Litany

As we look up at the starry sky at night, and as, in the morning, we see the landscape revealed as the sun dawns over the Earth—these experiences reveal a physical world but also a more profound world that

* cannot be bought with money,
* cannot be manufactured with technology,
* cannot be listed on the stock market,
* cannot be made in the chemical laboratory,
* cannot be reproduced with all our genetic engineering,
* cannot be sent by e-mail.

These experiences require only that we follow the deepest feelings of the human soul.

Closing Prayer

The Earth belongs to itself and to all the component members of the Earth community. The Earth is an entrancing celebration of existence in all its alluring qualities. Each earthly being participates in this cosmic celebration as the proper fulfillment of its powers of expression.

Thursday

The Great Work

Dawn

*The change has begun in every phase
of human activity.*

INVOCATION

History is governed by those overarching movements that give
shape and meaning to life by relating the human venture to
the larger destinies of the universe. Creating such a movement
might be called the *Great Work* of a people.

DOXOLOGY

The truly great society.
The society of the divine, the natural, and the human.
One energy shared by all three—a numinous psychic energy.

Opening Verse

The Earth is acting in us whenever we act.

Hymn

There is need for a great courtesy toward the Earth.
We are coming back to this once more
out of our new mode of understanding the universe.

We now experience ourselves as the latest arrivals,
after some 15 billion years of universe history
and after some 4.5 billion years of Earth history.

Here we are, born yesterday.

We need to present ourselves to the planet
as the planet presented itself to us,
in an evocatory rather than a dominating relationship.

There is need for a great courtesy toward the Earth.

Antiphon

The entire universe is involved in the healing of damaged
Earth.

Psalm

The work before us is the task,
not simply of ourselves,
but of the entire planet
and all its component members.

While the damage done
is immediately the work of the human,
the healing cannot be the work simply of the human
any more than the illness of some one organ of the body
can be healed simply through the efforts of that one organ.

Every member of the body
must bring about the healing.

So now the entire universe is involved
in the healing of damaged Earth,
more especially, of course, the forces of Earth
with the assistance of the light and warmth of the sun.

Psalm Prayer

We have indeed become strange beings, so completely are we at
odds with the planet that brought us into being. We dedicate
enormous talent and knowledge and research to developing a
human order disengaged from and even predatory on the very
sources whence we came and upon which we depend at every

moment of our existence. We have become insensitive toward the natural world and do not realize just what we are doing.

READING

The universe, Earth, life, and consciousness are all violent processes. The basic terms in cosmology, geology, biology, and anthropology all carry a heavy charge of tension and violence. Neither the universe as a whole nor any part of the universe is especially peaceful. As Heraclitus noted, "*Conflict is the father of all things.*"

The elements are born in supernovas. The sun is lit by gravitational pressures. The air we breathe and the water we drink come from the volcanic eruptions of gases from within the Earth. The mountains are formed by the clash of the great continental and oceanic segments of the Earth's crust. Life emerges and advances by the struggle of species for more complete life expression. Humans have made their way amid the harshness of the natural world and have imposed their violence on the natural world.

Among themselves humans have experienced unending conflict. An enormous psychic effort has been required to articulate the human mode of being in its full imaginative, emotional, and intellectual qualities, a psychic effort that emerges from and gives expression to that dramatic confrontation of forces that shape the universe. This confrontation may give rise to "*the tears of things,*" as described by Virgil, but its creative function would be difficult to ignore.

~Silence~

Versicle

We need not a human answer to an Earth problem,
but an Earth answer to an Earth problem.
The Earth will solve its problems, and possibly our own,
if we will let the Earth function in its own ways.
We need only listen to what the Earth is telling us.

Responsory

The present is not a time for desperation but for hopeful activity.

Canticle

None of our former revelatory experiences,
none of our renewal or rebirth rituals,
none of our apocalyptic descriptions
are quite adequate for this moment.

Their mythic power remains in a context
far removed from the power that is abroad in our world.

But even as we glance over the grimy world before us,
the sun shines radiantly over the Earth,
the aspen leaves shimmer in the evening breeze,
the coo of the mourning dove

and the swelling chorus of the insects fill the land,
while down in the hollows
the mist deepens the fragrance of the honeysuckle.

INTERCESSIONS

EVOCATION

We must feel that we are supported
by that same process that brought the Earth into being,
that power that spun the galaxies into space,
that lit the sun and brought the moon into its orbit.

Those same forces are still present;
indeed, we might feel their impact at this time
and understand that we are not isolated in the chill of space
with the burden of the future upon us
and without the aid of any other power.
We are supported by that power
that spun the galaxies into space.

CLOSING PRAYER

We cannot doubt that we have been given the intellectual vision, the spiritual insight, and even the physical resources we need for carrying out the transition that is demanded of these times, transition from the period when humans were a disruptive force on the planet Earth to the period when humans become present to the planet in a manner that is mutually enhancing.

Day

*In and through the Earth
spiritual energy is present.*

INVOCATION

The Great Work of a people is the work of all the people. No one is exempt. Each person in and through their personal work assists in the Great Work. Personal work needs to be aligned with the Great Work.

DOXOLOGY

The truly great society.
The society of the divine, the natural, and the human.
One energy shared by all three—a numinous psychic energy.

EXHORTATION

We must respond to the urgency of a renewal of the integral community of life systems throughout the Earth. Renewal is a community project.

ANTIPHON

Every member of the body must bring about the healing.

PSALM

We have silenced so many
of those wonderful voices of the universe
that once spoke to us of the grand mysteries of existence.
We no longer hear the voices of the rivers
or the mountains, or the voices of the sea.
The trees and meadows
are no longer intimate modes of spirit presence.

Everything about us
has become an *it* rather than a *thou*.

We continue to make music, write poetry,
and do our painting and sculpture and architecture,
but these activities easily become
an aesthetic expression simply of the human

and in time lose the intimacy and radiance
and awesome qualities of the universe itself.

We have, in the accepted universe of these times,
little capacity for participating in mysteries
celebrated in the earlier literary and artistic
and religious modes of expression.

For we could no longer live in the universe
in which these were written.
We could only look on, as it were.

PSALM PRAYER

We might remember that the reality of our own existence can be validated only in the context of honoring the larger communication that the natural world offers us in terms of wonder for the mind, beauty for the imagination, and intimacy for the emotions.

MEDITATION

A forceful presentation needs to be made to prevent the destruction of the divine image as presented to us in the created world, to prevent the wiping out of the source of our spiritual, intellectual, and aesthetic development, to prevent the burning away of irreplaceable resources for foolish and ephemeral purposes.

Reflection

Prayer

Our own future is inseparable from the future of the larger
community that brought us into being and sustains us in every
expression of our human quality of life, in our aesthetic and
emotional sensitivities, our intellectual perceptions, our sense
of the divine, as well as in our physical nourishment
and our bodily healing.

Lesson

No adequate scale of action can be expected until the human
community is able to act in some unified way to establish a
functional relation with the Earth process. The sea and air and
sky and sunlight and all living forms of Earth establish a single
planetary system. The human at the species level needs to fulfill
its functional role within this life community, for in the end the
human community will flourish or decline as the Earth and the
community of living species flourishes or declines.

Collect

The Earth acts in all that acts upon the Earth. The Earth is
acting in us whenever we act. What is clear is that the Earth
is mandating that the human community assume a responsibility never assigned to any previous generation. The human

community is passing from its stage of childhood into its adult stage of life. We must assume adult responsibilities.

Examen

We must wonder at ourselves and what we are doing and what is happening to the larger destinies of the Earth.

Recovery of Western civilization from its present addiction to use, as our primary relation to each other and to the world about us, must begin with the discovery of the world within, the world of the *psyche* as designated by the Greeks, a word translated by the term *anima* in the Latin world or by the term *soul* in the English world. The term *anima* is the word used to identify a living or animated or ensouled being from the earliest period in European thought. While the word *soul* has been abandoned by scientists lest it compromise the empirical foundations of their study, the reality of the thought expressed remains forever embedded in the very language that we use. The term *animal* will forever indicate an *ensouled* being. This interior world of the psyche—the anima, the soul, the spirit, or the mind—provides the basis for that interior presence that we experience with each other throughout the world of the living.

Confession

*   We can no longer hear the voice of the rivers, the mountains, or the sea:
    Earth Have Mercy

* The trees and meadows are no longer intimate modes
  of spirit presence:
  Cosmos Have Mercy

* The world about us has become an *it* rather than a
  thou:
  Earth Have Mercy

BENEDICTION

The universe story is our story,
individually and as the human community.
In this context we can feel secure
in our efforts to fulfill the Great Work before us.
The guidance, the inspiration
and the energy we need is available.
The accomplishment of the Great Work
is the task not simply of the human community
but of the entire planet Earth.
Even beyond Earth,
it is the Great Work of the universe itself.

Dusk

The world of mechanism has alienated us
from the wild beauty of the world about us.

INVOCATION

That the valley will be healed where it is damaged,
preserved in its present integrity
and renewed in its creative possibilities,
is the hope that is before us.

DOXOLOGY

The truly great society.
The society of the divine, the natural, and the human.
One energy shared by all three—a numinous psychic energy.

Opening Verse

Such an order of change, its nature and magnitude, has never before entered either into Earth history or human consciousness.

Hymn

After the distancing a new intimacy;
after the mechanistic
a greater biological sensitivity;
after damaging the Earth, a healing.
We need only look at the surrounding universe
in its more opaque material aspects—
look at it, listen to it, feel and experience
the full depths of its being.

Suddenly its opaque quality, its resistance,
falls away, and we enter into a world of mystery.
What seemed so opaque and impenetrable
suddenly becomes radiant with intelligibility,
powerful beyond imagination.

Antiphon

Moments of transformation are sacred moments.

Psalm I

Moments of transformation
are the mysterious, the sacred moments,
the moments when a numinous guidance shows through
amid the turbulent course of universe affairs.

Such moments we can no longer believe
are controlled by purely random consequences
out of a roiling sea of conflicting forces.
Between the random and the directed lies the creative.
Randomness is another name
for the mysterious ordering processes
that affect all artistic creativity.

Antiphon II

There must be a mystique of the rain.

Psalm II

A taste for existence
within the functioning of the natural world is urgent.
Without a fascination with the grandeur of the continent
the energy needed for its preservation will never be
    developed.

There must be a mystique of the rain
if we are ever to restore the purity of the rainfall.

This evocation of a mystique
is the role that is fulfilled by the poets.

Where the rainforests are being eliminated,
the soil eroded,
the mangrove swamps destroyed,
the coral reefs blasted,
the streams polluted,
there is a primary need to strengthen the mystique of the
    land.

Psalm Prayer

Fix our minds on the magnitude of the task before us. This task
concerns every member of the human community.

Epistle

Our difficulty is that we are just emerging from a technological
entrancement. During this period the human mind has been
placed within the narrowest confines it has experienced since
consciousness emerged. When a more expansive vision of the
human breaks upon us at this time, it should come as a shock,
as something unreal, insubstantial, unattainable.
Yet this is precisely what is happening. The excessive analytical
phase of science is over.

What is happening is something of a far greater magnitude.
It is a radical change in our mode of consciousness. Our challenge is to create a new language, even a new sense of what it

is to be human. It is to transcend not only national limitations, but even our species isolation, to enter into the larger community of living species. This brings about a completely new sense of reality and of value.

~Silence~

Responsory

Our challenge is to create a new language,
even a new sense of what it is to be human.

Canticle

For the children,
the children of every living being,
the children of the trees and grasses,
the children of the wolf,
the bear, and the cougar,
the children of the bluebird, the thrush,
and the great raptors that soar through the heavens,
the children of the salmon that begin and end their lives
in the upper reaches of the great western rivers,
the children, too, of human parents,
for all the children are born into a single sacred community.
None of the children nor any living being
throughout the entire planet has any integral future
except in alliance with every other being that finds its home
    here.

INTERCESSIONS

EVOCATION

We must feel that we are supported by that same process
that brought the Earth into being,
that power that spun the galaxies into space,
that lit the sun and brought the moon into its orbit.
Those same forces are still present;
indeed, we might feel their impact at this time
and understand that we are not isolated in the chill of space
with the burden of the future upon us
and without the aid of any other power.
We are supported by that power
that spun the galaxies into space.

CLOSING PRAYER

The trees will not be healthy if the rain is acid.
Nor will the soil be fertile.
Nor will humans have their proper nourishment.
Nor will imagination be activated to its grand poetic visions.
Nor will our sense of the divine be so exalted
if the Earth is diminished in its glory.
It is all quite clear. If we pull the threads, the fabric falls
    apart—
the human fabric, especially.

Dark

Our sense of who we are and what our role is
must begin
where the universe begins.

INVOCATION

Humans cannot simply do as they please with the natural world. Humans likewise cannot do as they please in relation to the psychic and spiritual forces of the world, but must enter into communion with these powers.

DOXOLOGY

The truly great society.
The society of the divine, the natural, and the human.

One energy shared by all three—
a numinous psychic energy.

Opening Verse

Every being exists in intimate relation with other beings and
in a constant exchange of gifts with each other.

Hymn

We begin to understand our human identity
with all the other modes of existence
that constitute with us the single universe community.

The one story includes us all.
We are, everyone, cousins to one another.
Every being is intimately present to
and immediately influencing every other being.

We see quite clearly that
what happens to the nonhuman happens to the human.
What happens to the outer world
happens to the inner world.
If the outer world is diminished in its grandeur
then the emotional, imaginative, intellectual,
and spiritual life of the human
is diminished or extinguished.
Without the soaring birds, the great forests,
the sounds and coloration of the insects,

the free-flowing streams, the flowering fields,
the sight of the clouds by day
and the stars at night,
we become impoverished
in all that makes us human.

There is now developing a profound mystique
of the natural world.

Beyond the technical comprehension of what is happening
and the directions in which we need to change,
we now experience the deep mysteries of existence
through the wonders of the world about us.

Antiphon

Whether we look down from the heavens or up at the sky.

Psalm

Our historical role in its deeper significance
has to do with a new understanding of the planet Earth:
This radiant blue-white planet hanging in the sky,
twirling upon its axis in the light of the sun each day,
swinging in its solar orbit each year.

Seven continents rise out of the great world ocean.
The polar regions appear as vast stretches of snow.
The Sierra Nevada along the western edge of the Americas,

the Alps in Europe, the Himalayas in Nepal,
T'ien Shan in China, Kilimanjaro in Africa—
these give to the continents a foreboding majesty.

The rivers flow down from the mountains
across the continents into the sea.
Rainforests girdle the planet in its equatorial regions.

Such vistas create an overwhelming impression
whether we look down from the heavens
or across the landscape
or up at the sky with its sun and clouds in the day
and its moon and stars in the night.

PSALM PRAYER

We seldom think about the Earth itself in its distinctive aspects;
we are enclosed so intimately within its fields and woodlands or
lost in the commercial frenzy of our cities. Only in recent times
have we experienced the Earth in its full spherical contours.

~SILENCE~

LITANY

Immediately present to our consciousness here on Earth are

* the landscape;
* the sky above,

* the Earth below;
* the grasses,
* the flowers,
* the forests,
* and the fauna—

Each in its own distinctive perfection fills our mind, our imagination, our emotional attraction.

CLOSING PRAYER

We are not lacking in the dynamic forces needed to create the future. We live immersed in a sea of energy beyond all comprehension. But this energy, in an ultimate sense, is ours not by domination but by invocation.

Desolation and Destiny

$\mathcal{D}$awn

The day of reckoning has come.

INVOCATION

We need guidance.
We need to go to the universe
and inquire concerning the basic issues of reality and value,
for, even more than the Earth,
the universe carries the deep mysteries
of our existence within itself.

DOXOLOGY

The universe is the primary sacred reality.
We become sacred by our participation
in this more sublime dimension of the world about us.

Opening Verse

When we destroy the living forms of this planet
we destroy modes of divine presence.

Hymn

The glory of the human
has become the desolation of Earth.
The desolation of Earth
is becoming the destiny of the human.

The historical mission of our times is:
To reinvent the human
At the species level
With critical reflection
Within the community of life systems
In a time-developmental context
By means of story and
Shared dream experience.

Antiphon I

Begin to recover a reverence for the material out of which we
were born.

Psalm

We now begin to realize
that the planet Earth will no longer endure

being despised or ignored
in its more integral being,
whether by scientists, technologists, or saints;
nor will it submit forever
to the abuse it has had to endure.

Already the Earth is taking away
the oxygen we breathe, the purity of the rain,
our protection from cosmic rays,
the careful balance of our climate,
the fruitfulness of the soil.

Begin to recover
a reverence for the material
out of which we were born,
for the nourishing context that sustains us,
the sounds and scenery,
the warmth of the wind
and the coolness of the water
all of which delight us and purify us
and communicate to us
some sense of sacred presence.

PSALM PRAYER

We no longer read the book of the universe.
Nor do we coordinate our world of human meaning
with the meaning of our surroundings.
We have disengaged from that profound interaction
with our environment inherent in our very nature.

Reading

Our present system, based on the plundering of the Earth's resources, is certainly coming to an end. It cannot continue. The industrial world on a global scale, as it functions presently, can be considered definitively bankrupt. There is no way out of the present recession within the context of our existing commercial-industrial processes. This recession is not only a financial recession or a human recession even. It is a recession of the planet itself. The Earth cannot sustain such an industrial system or its devastating technologies. In the future the industrial system will have its moments of apparent recovery, but these will be minor and momentary. The larger movement is toward dissolution. The impact of our present technologies is beyond what the Earth can endure.

Versicle

There is only one Earth community—one economic order, one health system, one moral order, one world of the sacred.

~Silence~

Responsory

All human institutions, professions, programs, and activities must now be judged primarily by the extent to which they inhibit, ignore, or foster a mutually enhancing human-Earth relationship.

CANTICLE

The time has now come
when we will listen or we will die.

The time has come to lower our voices,
to cease imposing our mechanistic patterns
on the biological processes of the Earth,
to resist the impulse to control,
to command, to force, to oppress,

and to begin quite humbly
to follow the guidance
of the larger community
on which all life depends.

INTERCESSIONS

EVOCATION

We must feel that we are supported
by that same process that brought the Earth into being,
that power that spun the galaxies into space,
that lit the sun and brought the moon into its orbit.

Those same forces are still present;
indeed, we might feel their impact at this time and
    understand
that we are not isolated in the chill of space

with the burden of the future upon us
and without the aid of any other power.
We are supported by that power
that spun the galaxies into space.

CLOSING PRAYER

The Earth community is a wilderness community that will not be bargained with. When this does take place in an abusive way, a vengeance awaits the human, for when the other living species are violated so extensively, the human itself is imperiled.

Day

Extinction is a difficult concept to grasp.

INVOCATION

Hear the creatures of Earth before it is too late,
before their voices are stilled forever through extinction.
Once gone, they will never be heard again.
Extinction is forever.

DOXOLOGY

The universe is the primary sacred reality.
We become sacred by our participation
in this more sublime dimension of the world about us.

Exhortation

We must reflect on what is happening. It is an urgent matter, especially for those of us who still live in a meaningful, even numinous, Earth community. We have not yet spoken. Nor even have we seen clearly what is happening. The issue goes far beyond economics, or commerce, or politics, or an evening of pleasantries as we look out over a scenic view. Something is happening beyond all this. We are losing splendid and intimate modes of divine presence. We are, perhaps, losing ourselves.

Antiphon II

Learn how to read the Great Book of Nature.

Psalm II

The peoples of the industrial world,
no longer live in a universe.
We live in a political world,
a nation, a business world, an economic order,
a cultural tradition, in Disney dreamland.

We live in cities, in a world of concrete and steel,
of wheels and wires, a world of business, of work.
We no longer see the stars at night
or the planets or the moon.

Even in the day we do not experience the sun
in any immediate or meaningful manner.

Summer and winter are the same inside the mall.
Ours is a world of highways,
parking lots, shopping centers.

We read books written
with a strangely contrived alphabet.

Our children do not learn how to read
the Great Book of Nature
or how to interact creatively
with the seasonal transformations of the planet.

They seldom learn
where their water comes from or where it goes.
We no longer coordinate our human celebration
with the great liturgy of the heavens.

Psalm Prayer

This is a bitter moment, not simply for the human, but for the
Earth itself. It is a bitter moment especially because our hopes
were so high, our arrogance unrestrained even by simple mod-
esty. It is a bitter moment because the origins of our actions
go so deep into our spiritual and cultural traditions, fostering
a sense that we were the measure of things.

Meditation

Reflect on what we have gained and what we have lost in the lifestyle that we have adopted; on the encompassing technocratic, manipulative world that we have established; even on the sense of religion that we have developed.

We witness the devastation we have wrought on this lovely continent, and even throughout the planet, and consider what we are now doing. We must reflect. We must reflect especially on the extinction of species we are bringing about.

The Divine experience they communicate will never again be available to humans. A dimension of the human soul will never be activated as it might have been. None of the wonders of the human can replace what we are losing. We have lost sight of the fact that these myriad creatures are revelations of the divine and inspirations to our spiritual life.

Prayer

Appreciate the planet that provides us with a world abundant in the volume and variety of food for our nourishment, a world exquisite in supplying beauty of form, sweetness of taste, delicate fragrances for our enjoyment, and exciting challenges for us to overcome with skill and action.

It is this renewed energy of reciprocity with nature, in all its complexity and remarkable beauty, that can help provide the psychic and spiritual energies necessary for the work ahead.

Lesson

We have subverted the basic biological law that every life-form shall have other life-forms or conditions that limit its expansion, so that no single life-form or group of life-forms should suffocate the other life-forms. The power of our technologies is now such, however, that nature cannot prevent us from doing whatever we decide in diminishing the splendor and vigor and variety of life upon the Earth.

Nature has its own technologies. The entire hydrological cycle can even be regarded as a huge engineering project, a project vastly greater than anything humans could devise with such beneficent consequences throughout the life systems of the planet. We can differentiate between an acceptable human technology and an unacceptable human technology quite simply: An acceptable one is compatible with the integral functioning of the technologies governing the natural systems; an unacceptable one is incompatible with the technologies of the natural world.

Collect

We have during these past two centuries severely damaged our planet with massive technological strategies and machines. That these innovations do much good is surely true; that they have a demonic aspect is also true.

Examen

We must wonder at ourselves and what we are doing and what is happening to the larger destinies of the Earth.

The difficulty presently is with the mechanistic fixation in the human psyche, in our emotions and sensitivities as well as our minds. Even when we recognize our intimacy, our family relations with all the forms of existence about us, we cannot speak to those forms.

Confession

* Traditional religion, alienated from the modern world, has reached a spiritual impasse:
  Earth Have Mercy

* It has shown neither the intelligence nor the willingness to walk with us through this modern period in our splendor and in our shame:
  Cosmos Have Mercy

* Religion has not fully communicated the vital spiritual nourishment and illumination needed by a suffering world:
  Earth Have Mercy

BENEDICTION

The story of the past provides our most secure basis of hope that the Earth will so guide us through the peril of the present that we may provide a fitting context for the next phase of the emergent mystery of earthly existence. That the guidance is available we cannot doubt. The difficulty is in the order of magnitude of change that is required of us.

Dusk

Planet Earth is a one-time project.
There is no real second chance.

INVOCATION

Assistance from the entire universe is needed if a person is to
have both the psychic and the physical powers needed to live
through the perils of earthly existence.

DOXOLOGY

The universe is the primary sacred reality.
We become sacred by our participation
in this more sublime dimension of the world about us.

Opening Verse

The Earth entire and the human community are bound in a single destiny, and that destiny just now has a disintegrating aspect.

Hymn

We now have a disturbed biosphere
brought about by a technology
for which nature has no limiting forces
short of suffocating the human perpetrators
with their own waste products.

Antiphon I

If we were truly moved by the beauty of the world.

Psalm I

If we were truly moved
by the beauty of the world about us,
we would honor the Earth in a profound way.

We would understand immediately
and turn away with a certain horror
from all those activities
that violate the integrity of the planet.
That we have not done so

reveals that the disturbance exists
at a more basic level of consciousness
and on a greater order of magnitude
than we dare admit to ourselves or even think about.

This unprecedented pathology
is not merely in those more immediate forms
of economic activity that have done such damage;

it is even more deeply embedded in our cultural traditions,
in our religious traditions,
in our very language,
in our entire value systems.

Antiphon II

If there were a parliament of creatures.

Psalm II

The day of reckoning has come.

In this disintegrating phase of our industrial society,
we now see ourselves not as the splendor of creation,
but as the most pernicious mode of earthly being.

We are the termination,
not the fulfillment of the Earth process.

If there were a parliament of creatures,
its first decision might well be
to vote the humans out of the community,
too deadly a presence to tolerate any further.

We are the affliction of the world, its demonic presence.
We are the violation of Earth's most sacred aspects.

PSALM PRAYER

Listen with attention and a willingness to respond to the Earth's demands that we cease our industrial assault, that we abandon our rage against the conditions of our earthly existence, that we renew our human participation in the grand Liturgy of the universe.

EPISTLE

Whatever joy we may have in life, there is also a deep sense of tragedy built into our experience of ourselves and the world in which we exist. In its raw, uncultivated state, the human being is not satisfactory. The human condition is experienced as thoroughly and absolutely unsatisfactory. It must be altered to a degree so great that it is described as a new birth, a truly human and spiritual birth. Otherwise, the first birth never comes to term but is cut off in an undeveloped, savage condition.

How to sustain the pain of existence meanwhile, how to give it meaning, then how to bring it under the influence of a transforming saving discipline: These are the basic challenges.

Traditional religions consider that all the forces in heaven and Earth must contribute to this transforming process, to this new birth. This is the meaning of initiation rituals found among Indigenous peoples, of the Hindu bestowal of the sacred cord, and of Christian baptism. This sense of giving a new birth to individuals and the community is the essential doctrine of Marxist socialism, as well.

In the traditional period, there was general agreement that this new birth brought us into a higher, sacred, or spiritual order that radiates over the whole of life and gives sublime meaning to every last detail of human existence. The larger purpose of life is to bring this spiritual birth to its full expression. It is not just salvation from the human condition—it is the transformation of the human condition itself.

~SILENCE~

RESPONSORY

What, then, is needed? A modern world responsive to the spiritual and spiritual traditions responsive to the modern world. These must be mutually enfolded in the common task of bringing us to our full birth as human beings.

CANTICLE

We have heard Bach's Passion
The Lamentations of Jeremiah

Ancient experiences of darkness over the Earth,
Light born anew.

But now, darkness deeper than even God
can reach with a quick healing power.

What sound,
What song,
What cry appropriate—

What cry can bring a healing
When a million-year rainfall
Can hardly wash away the life-destroying stain?

What sound?
Listen—Earth sound.
Listen—the wind through the hemlock.
Listen—the owl's soft hooting in the winter night.
Listen—the wolf—wolf song.

Cry of distant meanings
woven into a seamless sound.
Never before has the cry of the wolf
expressed such meaning on the winter mountainside.

This cry, our revelation
As the sun sinks lower in the sky
Over our wounded world.

The meaning of the moment
And the healing of the wound
Are there in a single cry.

A throat open wide
For the wild sacred sound
Of some Great Spirit
A Gothic sound—come down from the beginning of time.

If only humans could hear, now see, the wolf
as guardian spirit
as savior guide?

Our Jeremiah, telling us,
not about the destruction of
Jerusalem or its temple

Our Augustine, telling us,
not about the destruction of Rome and civilization

Our Bach,
telling us not about the Passion of Christ in ancient times,
But about the Passion of Earth in our times?

Wolf—our Earth, our Christ, ourselves.

The arch of the Cathedral itself takes on the shape
Of the uplifted throat of the wolf
Lamenting our present destiny

Beseeching humankind
To bring back the sun
To let the flowers bloom in the meadows,
The rivers run through the hills
And let the Earth
And all its living creatures
Live their
Wild,
Fierce,
Serene
And Abundant life.

INTERCESSIONS

EVOCATION

We are supported
by that same process
that brought the Earth into being,
that power that spun the galaxies into space,
that lit the sun and brought the moon into its orbit.
Those same forces are still present;
We feel their impact and understand
that we are not isolated in the chill of space
with the burden of the future upon us
and without the aid of any other power.
We are supported by that power
that spun the galaxies into space.

CLOSING PRAYER

If we lived in a less resplendent world, our sense of the divine would itself be diminished. As we lose our experience of the songbirds, our experience of the butterflies, the flowers in the fields, the trees and woodlands, the streams that pour over the land and the fish that swim in their waters; as we lose our experience of these things our imagination suffers in proportion, as do our feelings and even our intelligence.

Dark

Sometimes we appear as the peril of the planet,
if not its tragic fate.

INVOCATION

Modern experiences of social anarchy, deconstruction,
and the radical absurdity of all existence
are a preparatory phase,
an effort at total honesty,
a purifying of our illusions,
and thus, at least, a beginning.

DOXOLOGY

The universe is the primary sacred reality.
We become sacred by our participation
in this more sublime dimension of the world about us.

Opening Verse

The entire planet is a single organic reality that needs to be addressed in its spirit and person qualities as well as in its physical aspects.

Hymn

We cannot discover ourselves
without first discovering the universe,
the Earth, and the imperatives of our own being.
Each of these has a creative power and a vision
far beyond any rational thought
or cultural creation of which we are capable.
Nor should we think of these
as isolated from our own individual being
or from the human community.
We have no existence except
within the Earth and within the universe.

Antiphon

How great a privilege it is to be living on this luxuriant planet.

Psalm

Much could be said about what it would be like
to be without our emotional or aesthetic
or religious development, to be without the images

evoked by the various physical phenomena—
by the clouds, the rains, and the wind;
by the mountains, rivers, and valleys;
as well as by all living forms.

Our explorations of the moon should be sufficient
to convince us how great a privilege it is
to be living on this luxuriant planet.

We tend to emphasize
the resplendence of the Earth
as seen from the moon.

Yet we fail to reflect adequately
on the desolate future there would be for the human
if we were reduced to the lunar mode of being.

The lunar landscape may confront us
with its barrenness and remind us
of all that is so alive and exciting on Earth.

We might wonder what it would be like
if we had existed first on the moon
and then came to the planet Earth.

The experience would be so overwhelming
that we could not absorb the impact of Earth's beauty.

Psalm Prayer

As we bring about the poisoning of air, soil, sea, and all living beings inhabiting these regions, we begin to make the Earth a place where the existence of higher life forms is threatened on a planetary scale.

~Silence~

Litany

The book of vertebrates includes some eight hundred species of higher animals that are presently imperiled in their wilderness habit. The listing includes some of the most gorgeous expressions of life that have ever been present on the Earth:

* the great whales, the Asian elephants,
* the magnificent snow leopard,
* the polar bear, the grizzly bear,
* the jaguar, the cheetah,
* the California pronghorn antelope,
* the giant ibis, the California condor,
* the black-necked swan,
* the whooping crane,
* the Mississippi sandhill crane,
* the golden eagle, the southern bald eagle,
* the paradise parrot, the ivory-billed woodpecker.

The list could go on and on merely among the vertebrates, but then we would need to begin the list of those splendid insects upon which so much of life depends, and then the plant world, especially the flowering plants that are endangered, and the woodlands. The list could go on and on.

Closing Prayer

The Great Work.

That we will succeed is to some extent assured by the whole of past history, by the forces that sent the galaxies into space, that shaped Earth and brought forth living creatures in the sea, on Earth, and in the sky. It is to some extent also assured by the course of human history with all its agonies and catastrophic periods. We cannot expect to achieve anything substantial without upheaval. Its full dimensions we do not know. The future is also hopeful because of the integral, cosmological story available to us now for the first time.

Pax Gaia

Dawn

*Bring back the ancient symbol of the universe
as the Great Mother.*

INVOCATION

Our long motherless period may be coming to a close; hopefully, the long period of our mistreatment of planet Earth is being terminated.

DOXOLOGY

This is the proper role of the Great Mother:
to be the primordial source
whence the vast diversity of beings in the universe
comes into existence.

Opening Verse

We are members of the great universe community.
We participate in its life.
We are nourished by this community,
instructed by this community,
governed by this community,
and healed by this community.
In and through this community
we enter into communion with that numinous mystery
whence all things depend for their existence and their
    activity.

Hymn

The universe is a single gorgeous celebratory event.

We are returning to the primordial community
of the universe, the Earth, and all living beings.
Each has its own voice, its role, its power over the whole.

Each has its special symbolism.
The excitement of life
is in the numinous experience
wherein we are given to each other
in the largest celebration of existence
in which all things attain their highest expression,
for the universe, by definition,
is a single gorgeous celebratory event.

Antiphon

The natural world is the maternal source
of our being as Earthlings.

Psalm

The natural world is not simply object,
not simply a usable thing,
not an inert mode of being
awaiting its destiny
to be manipulated by the divine
or exploited by the human.

The natural world is subject as well as object.

The natural world is the maternal source
of our being as Earthlings
and the life-giving nourishment
of our physical, emotional, aesthetic,
moral, and religious existence.

The natural world
is the larger sacred community
to which we belong.

To be alienated from this community
is to become destitute
in all that makes us human.

To damage this community is to diminish our own existence.

Psalm Prayer

What is needed is a new spiritual, even mystical, communion with Earth, a true aesthetic of Earth, sensitivity to Earth's needs, a valid economy of Earth.

Reading

Earlier peoples saw in natural phenomena something of a real world, an abiding world, a world beyond this ephemeral appearance, a world imaged forth in the wonders of the sun and clouds by day and the stars and planets by night, a world normative for us here on Earth, a world that enfolded the human in some profound manner.

This other world was the guardian, the teacher, the healer, the source whence humans were born, were nourished, protected, guided—the destiny to which we returned.

Above all, the surrounding world provided the psychic power we needed in our moments of crisis. Together with the visible world, this other world and the human world, we formed a meaningful threefold community of existence.

This other world was the guardian, the teacher, the healer, the source whence humans were born, were nourished, protected, guided—the destiny to which we returned.

VERSICLE

The Peace of Earth—not simply *Pax Romana* or *Pax Humana*, but *Pax Gaia*, the Peace of Earth, the ancient mythic name for the planet.

This is the original and final peace, the peace granted by whatever power it is that brings our world into being. Within the universe, the planet Earth with all its wonder is the place for the meeting of the divine and the human.

~SILENCE~

RESPONSORY

While we emerge into being from within the Earth process and enable the universe to come to itself in a special mode of psychic intimacy, it is evident that we have also a special power over the universe in its earthly expression.

CANTICLE

Look up at the sky—
the heavens so blue,
the sun so radiant,
the clouds so playful!

The soaring raptors,
woodland creatures,

meadows in bloom,
rivers singing their way to the sea.

Wolfsong on the land,
whalesong in the sea,
celebration everywhere—
wild, riotous!

Immense as a monsoon
lifting an ocean of joy
then spilling it down over
the Appalachian landscape
drenching us all
in a deluge of delight.

As we open our arms and
rush toward each other,
all of us moved by that vast
compassionate curve
that brings all things together
in intimate celebration—

Celebration that is the universe itself.

INTERCESSIONS

EVOCATION

We must feel that we are supported
by that same process that brought the Earth into being,

that power that spun the galaxies into space,
that lit the sun and brought the moon into its orbit.
Those same forces are still present;
indeed, we might feel their impact at this time
and understand that we are not isolated
in the chill of space with the burden of the future upon us
and without the aid of any other power.
We are supported by that power that spun the galaxies into
   space.

Closing Prayer

Honor the beings layered throughout the natural world—the winged creatures, four-legged creatures, insects, and all realms of life.

Honor relationships with the rain and the winds, with the mountains, the valleys, the plants, the animals, the homelands, the stars, and the sun in the heavens.

Honor personal intimacy with cosmic powers.

Day

*The Earth seems to be rising
in defense of herself and her children
after this long period of patriarchal
domination.*

INVOCATION

Whatever is done by the power that brought the universe into
being is done primarily for the perfection of the entire creation,
not for any individual within creation. Thus revelation, Incar-
nation, and Redemption are primarily for the entire universe,
not primarily for any group or individual being within the
universe.

DOXOLOGY

This is the proper role of the Great Mother:
to be the primordial source
whence the vast diversity of beings in the universe
comes into existence.

EXHORTATION

We came into being within the life community through the
billions of years that it took to shape a world into which humans could be born. It has been a creative maternal process
throughout, with all the violence of the primordial fireball, the
supernova explosions, and the volcanic eruptions from within
the Earth itself. However terrifying these transition moments,
they have consistently been birth moments.

ANTIPHON

The great spiritual traditions of humankind represent cosmic
powers.

PSALM

The great spiritual traditions of humankind
emerged out of a confrontation with terror.
These traditions are not ephemeral activities
of weak souls with little of that basic courage
required to deal with fundamental life issues.

These spiritual traditions represent
humanity's ultimate confrontation with chaos,
with incoherence, with destruction, with the absurd.

These are not abstractions, but cosmic powers
vastly different and infinitely more effective,
more devastating, and more pervasive
than those forces we generally think of
when considering the evils to which humans are subject.

PSALM PRAYER

Archetypal symbols are the main instruments for the evocation
of the energies needed for the future renewal of the Earth. They
provide not only the understanding and the sense of direction
that we need; they also evoke the energy needed to create this
new situation. The organic unity and creative power of the
planet Earth is expressed in the symbol of the Great Mother.

MEDITATION

The Divine Mother symbolism so widespread throughout the
world (especially in the Near Eastern civilizations and in India) helped cultures deal with the immense universe and the
sense of personal isolation. In China, the Tao was seen more
as Divine Mother than as Ruling Father. In East Asia, Kuan
Yin, originally a masculine savior divinity, was gradually altered
into a feminine figure, to provide for those deeper needs that
humans feel for a compassionate heavenly personality bending
down over the world of human affliction.

This awareness of feminine affection and concern as a supreme revelation of being came upon the world with great power and removed the destructive experience humans had of themselves and of the universe in which they lived.

Such creative, redemptive, and bliss-bestowing deities dwelt in great shrines before which humans could stand and feel themselves in the presence of that which fulfills their most fundamental needs and their most sublime spiritual longings.

Humans participated in a divine order of things, felt its healing pour over them, and realized that they were much more than insignificant creatures tossed about in an uncertain and meaningless universe.

Prayer

We might hope that what we are now experiencing is another birth moment, yet the patriarchal period is too poignant in its past memories and its present realities for us to fully understand what is happening or what will emerge in the years to come.

Lesson

The genius of our times is to join the physical identification, experience, and understanding of the Earth, given by scientific inquiry, with the traditional mythic symbols and rituals associated with the Great Mother.

To appreciate both of these in their proper relationship is to overcome our alienation from the universe and from the Earth.

This understanding should evoke the emotional and imaginative sympathies needed for the sensitive care humans need to give to the natural world and also provide for our aesthetic excitement and celebration of the natural world.

COLLECT

For in the end the universe
can only be explained in terms of celebration.
It is all an exuberant expression of existence itself.

EXAMEN

We must wonder at ourselves and what we are doing and what is happening to the larger destinies of the Earth.

We live in a human world, a world where all our values are human. The natural world is experienced as subservient to the human. Its reality has diminished as the human has been magnified. If we give attention to the universe, it is to the scholarly world of scientific equations, of atomic and subatomic particles; to the technological world of mechanistic contrivances; to the economic world of unlimited human use of the Earth as a collection of natural resources.

CONFESSION

* The Earth continues to disintegrate under the plundering assault of humans:
Earth Have Mercy

* We still do not feel that we should revere every living creature—from the lowliest insect to the great eagle in the sky:
Cosmos Have Mercy

* We fail to recognize our obligation to bow before the majesty of the mountains and rivers, the forests, the grasslands, the deserts, the coastlands:
Earth Have Mercy

BENEDICTION

We cannot discover ourselves without first discovering the universe, the Earth, and the imperatives of our own being. Each of these has a creative power and a vision far beyond any rational thought or cultural creation of which we are capable. Nor should we think of these as isolated from our own individual being or from the human community.

We have no existence except within the Earth and within the universe.

Dusk

Restore a sense of the Earth as matrix of the human.

INVOCATION

The universe is the primary locus, the primary place for the meeting of the Divine and the human.

DOXOLOGY

This is the proper role of the Great Mother:
to be the primordial source
whence the vast diversity of beings in the universe
comes into existence.

Opening Verse

The Peace of Earth is indivisible. The Earth is a single organic reality that must survive in its integrity. The cosmology of peace is the basic issue.

Hymn

Earth's Desire:

To be seen in her loveliness
to be tasted in her delicious fruits
to be listened to in her teaching
to be endured in the severity of her discipline
to be experienced as the maternal source
whence we come and
the destiny to which we return.

Antiphon

Our greatest resource for peace.

Psalm

We cannot be fully nourished
in the depths of our being
if we try to isolate ourselves individually

or if we seek to deprive others of their share
by increasing our own;
for the food that we eat nourishes us
in both our souls and our bodies.

To eat alone is to be starved in some part of our being.
We need to reflect that our individual delight
in the song of the birds
or the sound of the crickets and cicadas in the evening
is enhanced, not diminished,
when we listen together in the evening,
with our families and our friends.
We experience an easing of the tensions
that develop between us,
for the songs that we hear draw us
into the intimacy of the same psychic space.
So too music—our folk music
as well as the symphonies of Mozart or Beethoven—
draws an unlimited number of persons
into the same soul space.

Perhaps our greatest resource for peace
is in an awareness that we enrich ourselves
when we share our possessions with others.

We discover peace when we learn
to esteem those goods whereby we benefit ourselves
in proportion as we give them to others.

Antiphon II

Our greatest source of creative energy.

Psalm II

Acceptance of the challenging aspect
of the natural world
is a primary condition for creative intimacy
with the natural world.

Without this opaque
or even threatening aspect of the universe
we would lose our greatest source of creative energy.
This opposing element is as necessary for us
as is the weight of the atmosphere that surrounds us.

This containing element, even the gravitation
that binds us to the Earth,
should be experienced as liberating and energizing,
rather than confining.

Psalm Prayer

The very structure and functioning of the universe and of the
planet Earth reveal an indescribable diversity bound in an all-
embracing unity. The heavens themselves are curved over the
Earth in an encompassing embrace.

Epistle

The subject with which we are concerned is the spirituality of the Earth. By this I do not mean a spirituality that is directed toward an appreciation of the Earth. I speak of the Earth as subject, not as object. I am concerned with the maternal principle out of which we were born and whence we derive all that we are and all that we have. In our totality we are born of the Earth. We are Earthlings. The Earth is our origin, our nourishment, our support, our guide. Our spirituality itself is Earth-derived. If there is no spirituality in the Earth, then there is no spirituality in ourselves. The human and the Earth are totally implicated each in the other. Not to recognize the spirituality of the Earth is to indicate a radical lack of spiritual perception in ourselves.

~Silence~

Responsory

There is now only one issue before us, the issue of survival, not merely physical survival, but survival in a world of fulfillment, survival in a living world, where the violets bloom in the springtime, where the stars shine down in all their mystery, survival in a world of meaning.

Canticle

As humans we are born of the Earth,
nourished by the Earth, healed by the Earth.

The natural world tells us:
I will feed you, I will clothe you,
I will shelter you, I will heal you.

Only do not so devour me or use me
that you destroy my capacity
to mediate the divine and the human.

For I offer you a communion with the divine,
I offer you gifts
that you can exchange with each other,
I offer you flowers
whereby you may express your reverence
for the divine and your love for each other.

In the vastness of the sea,
in the snow-covered mountains,
in the rivers flowing through the valleys,
in the serenity of the landscape,
and in the foreboding of the great storms
that sweep over the land,

in all these experiences
I offer you inspiration
for your music, for your art, your dance.

INTERCESSIONS

EVOCATION

We are supported
by that same process
that brought the Earth into being,
that power that spun the galaxies into space,
that lit the sun and brought the moon into its orbit.
Those same forces are still present;
We feel their impact and understand
that we are not isolated in the chill of space
with the burden of the future upon us
and without the aid of any other power.
We are supported by that power
that spun the galaxies into space.

CLOSING PRAYER

In our contemplation of how tragic moments of disintegration over the course of the centuries were followed by immensely creative moments of renewal, we receive our great hope for the future. To initiate and guide this next creative moment of the story of the Earth is the Great Work of the religions of the world as we move on into the future.

Dark

*Every atomic particle is immediately present to
every other atomic particle in a manner that
enables us to say that the volume of each atom
is the volume of the universe.*

INVOCATION

The evolutionary process
is from the beginning
a spiritual as well as a physical process.

DOXOLOGY

This is the proper role of the Great Mother:
to be the primordial source
whence the vast diversity of beings in the universe
comes into existence.

Opening Verse

In the emerging Ecozoic Era, all the archetypes
of the collective unconscious will attain a new validity
as well as new patterns of functioning,
especially in our understanding of the death-rebirth symbol
and the symbols of the heroic journey, the Great Mother,
the tree of life.

Hymn

The universe expresses itself
in the blazing radiance of the stars
and in the vast reaches of the galactic systems.

Its most intimate expression of itself, however,
is in this tiny planet: a planet that could not exist
in its present form except in a universe such as this one,
in which it has emerged and from which
it has received its life energies.

The planet presents itself to us,
not as a uniform global reality,
but as a complex of highly differentiated regions
caught up in the comprehensive unity
of the planet itself.

There are arctic and tropical,
coastal and inland regions,

mountains and plains,
river valleys and deserts.
Each of these regions
has its distinctive geological formation,
climatic conditions, and living forms.

Together these constitute
the wide variety of life communities
that may be referred to as bioregions.
Each is coherent within itself
and intimately related to the others.
Together they express the wonder and splendor
of this garden planet of the universe.

Antiphon

Every being in the universe
articulates some special quality of the universe.

Psalm

The human is neither an addendum
nor an intrusion into the universe.
We are quintessentially integral with the universe.

In ourselves, the universe is revealed to itself
as we are revealed in the universe.

Every being in the universe articulates
some special quality of the universe
in its entirety.

Nothing in the universe could be itself
apart from every other being in the universe,
nor could any moment of the universe story exist
apart from all other moments in the story.

Yet it is within our own being
that we have our own unique experience
of the universe and of the Earth in its full reality.

Psalm Prayer

The human is less a being on the Earth or in the universe than
a dimension of the Earth and indeed of the universe itself. The
shaping of our human mode of being depends on the support
and guidance of this comprehensive order of things—this comprehensive source. Nor is this source distant from us.

~Silence~

Litany

What do you see?

* What do you see when you look up at the sky at night?
* When you see the blazing stars against the midnight
  heavens?

* What do you see when the dawn breaks over the eastern horizon?
* What are your thoughts in the fading days of summer as the birds depart on their southward journey,
* Or when the leaves turn brown and are blown away?
* What are your thoughts when you look out over the ocean in the evening?

What do you see?

CLOSING PRAYER

Soon the late summer moon
will give a light sheen to the landscape.
Something of a dream experience.
Perhaps on occasion we participate
in the original *Dream of the Earth*.
Perhaps there are times
when this primordial design becomes visible,
as in a palimpsest, when we remove the later imposition.

The Dream of the Earth.

Where else can we go for the guidance needed
for the task that is before us?

Toward the Ecozoic

Dawn

The future must be felt as already present.

INVOCATION

This present world, so far distinguished by its science and technology, must now become distinguished by its spiritual depth and the richness of its human qualities. It must in some manner make present the paradisal aspects of the eschatological community.

DOXOLOGY

We are experiencing a moment of grace.
Such moments are privileged moments.
The great transformations of the universe occur at such times.
The present is one of those moments of transformation.

Opening Verse

The ecological age fosters the deep awareness
of the sacred presence within each reality of the universe.

Hymn

There is an awe and reverence
due to the stars in the heavens,
the sun, and all heavenly bodies;
to the seas and the continents;
to all living forms of trees and flowers;
to the myriad expressions of life in the sea;
to the animals of the forests and the birds of the air.

To wantonly destroy a living species
is to silence forever a divine voice.
Our primary need for the various life-forms of the planet
is a psychic, rather than a physical, need.

The ecological age seeks to establish and maintain
this subjective identity, this authenticity
at the heart of every being.

Antiphon

In the beginning was the dream.

Psalm

In the beginning was the dream.
Through the dream all things were made,
and without the dream nothing was made
that has been made.
While all things share in this dream,
as humans we share in this dream in a special manner.

This is the entrancement,
the magic of the world about us,
its mystery, its ineffable quality.

What primordial source could,
with no model for guidance,
imagine such a fantastic world
as that in which we live—
the shape of the orchid,
the coloring of the fish in the sea,
the winds and the rain,
the variety of sounds that flow over the Earth,
the resonant croaking of the bullfrogs,
the songs of the crickets,
and the pure joy of the predawn singing of the mockingbird?

Psalm Prayer

The excitement of life and the sustaining psychic vigor are
evoked by our participation in this magnificent process. The

human is that being in whom this grand diversity of the universe celebrates itself in conscious self-awareness.

READING

Here we find the sublime expression of the deepest mystery of the universe: the revelation of the divine. To deepen this experience of the divine is one of the purposes of all spiritual discipline, all spiritual experience. This sense of communion at the heart of reality is the central force bringing the ecological age into existence. Thus, the birth of a new overwhelming spiritual experience at this moment of Earth history.

VERSICLE

Religion is born out of the sense of wonder and awe of the majesty and fearsomeness of the universe itself. These experiences evoke in the human soul a sense of mystery and admiration, veneration and worship—recognition of the Divine manifested in nature.

~SILENCE~

RESPONSORY

Only religious forces can move human consciousness at the depth needed. Only religious forces can sustain the effort that will be required over the long period of time during which adjustment must be made. Only religion can measure the magnitude of what we are about.

CANTICLE

The gravitation that pervades the universe,
holds it together, and causes each tiniest particle
to attract and be attracted to every other particle,
involves an awareness, an inner communication,
an intercommunion.

This is why the attraction of gravitation
that brings about the concentration of atoms
which causes such enormous heat
within the various celestial bodies
is a remarkable symbol of love in the human order.

Only such love can sustain the human effort
and call forth those vast energies needed to create
the world of the future.

INTERCESSIONS

EVOCATION

We must feel that we are supported
by that same process that brought the Earth into being,
that power that spun the galaxies into space,

that lit the sun and brought the moon into its orbit.
Those same forces are still present;
indeed, we might feel their impact at this time
and understand that we are not isolated
in the chill of space with the burden of the future upon us
and without the aid of any other power.
We are supported by that power
that spun the galaxies into space.

Closing Prayer

In moments of confusion such as the present, we are not left simply to our own rational contrivances. We are supported by the ultimate powers of the universe as they make themselves present to us through the spontaneities within our own beings. We need only become sensitized to these spontaneities, not with a naive simplicity, but with critical appreciation. This intimacy with our genetic endowment, and through this endowment with the larger cosmic process, is not primarily the role of the philosopher, priest, prophet, or professor. It is the role of the shamanic personality, a type that is emerging once again in our society.

Day

The Great Wheel Turns.
The Great Cosmic Wheel of the Universe.
One energy shared by all.
A numinous psychic energy.

INVOCATION

We need the guidance of the prophet, the priest, the saint, the yogi, the Buddhist monk, the Chinese sage, the Greek philosopher, and the modern scientists. We need an ecological spirituality with an integral ecologist to serve as spiritual guide for these times.

DOXOLOGY

We are experiencing a moment of grace.
Such moments are privileged moments.

The great transformations of the universe occur at such
  times.
The present is one of those moments of transformation.

Exhortation

Humans cannot long sustain alienation from the ecstatic bliss
that is the culmination of all great cultural traditions. If this is
not granted in the immediacy of the present in its legitimate
reality, then we will seek illusory fulfillment in whatever ways
are available to us. We must live in paradise not tomorrow but
today.

Antiphon

Each individual is expressing the Divine perfection.

Psalm

Every being is a unique being.

There are no two realities the same.
There are no two leaves on a tree the same.
There are no two drops of rain, no two snowflakes,
no two atoms, no two of anything that are the same.
Sameness is a deficiency.
It is the uniqueness that establishes the high value of things
so that each being contributes something to the universe
that no other being ever could contribute or ever will
  contribute.

Difference is primary, and in the human order,
difference is such that each individual seems almost
to be a different species.

And the sacred part of every being—
of every atom, of every molecule, of every bird,
of every tree, of every leaf even
is that each brings something to the universe that is unique,
that is not repeatable.
If we do not realize the possibilities within ourselves
as individuals, something is lacking in the universe
that can never be replaced.
There is a failure, so to speak, that is beyond remedy,
because no one else will ever be able to do
what each individual is called to do.

Each individual is expressing the Divine perfection
in a unique way,
and to carry that uniqueness to its full expression
is the obligation of each individual being.

Psalm Prayer

What must be sought for is the recovery, through critical processes, of a second naïveté, an earlier interior experience of a harmonious and luminous universe, associated by the Chinese with the *lost mind of the child.*

Meditation

We might go to the desert, or high in the mountains, or to the seashores, where we might really see, perhaps for the first time, the dawn appear in the eastern sky—its first faint purple glow spreading over the horizon, then the slow emergence of the great golden sphere. In the evening, we might see the flaming sunset in the west. We might see the stars come down from the distant heavens and present themselves almost within reach of our arms if we stood on tiptoe.

So too, we might begin to view the change of the seasons: the springtime awakening of the land as the daisies bloom in the meadows and the dogwood tree puts forth its frail white blossoms. We might experience the terrifying moments when summer storms break over the horizon and lightning streaks across the sky, the moments when darkness envelops us in the deep woodlands, or when we experience the world about us as a vast array of powers asserting themselves. When we view all this, we might begin to imagine our way into the future.

Prayer

The natural world itself is our primary language as it is our primary scripture, our primary awakening to the mysteries of existence. Learn what we are being told by unmediated experience of the world about us.

LESSON

A spirituality suited to contemporary humans must rest on the drive we feel for a total experience of the universe. This is what propels us into the primordial past as into the distant future, into the outer dimensions of the universe as well as into the fantastic worlds hidden in the smallest particles of matter. We must walk on the moon both as a physical experience and as a mystical symbol of our inner journey. This drive toward fulfillment includes the quest to understand the deepest realms of the unconscious self as they are indicated by symbols revealed in dreams. This search into the deepest origins of psychic experience reveals that as humans we are centered in our place within the whole of things; the individual person seeks the reality of the whole and the whole of reality.

COLLECT

We need an ecological spirituality with an integral ecologist as spiritual guide. The great mission of the present is to renew all the traditional religious-spiritual traditions in the context of the integral functioning of the biosystems of the planet.

EXAMEN

We must wonder at ourselves and what we are doing and what is happening to the larger destinies of the Earth.
   A primary allegiance to this larger community is needed. It

will do little good for any nation to seek its own well-being by destroying the very conditions for planetary survival.

This larger vision is no longer utopian. It directly concerns the hardest, most absolute reality there is: the reality of the water we drink, the air we breathe, the food we eat.

CONFESSION

* We have changed the very chemistry of the planet:
  Earth Have Mercy

* We have altered the biosystem, the topography, and even the geological structure of the planet:
  Cosmos Have Mercy

* We have changed structures and functions that have taken hundreds of millions and even billions of years to bring into existence:
  Earth Have Mercy

BENEDICTION

The response that we give must have a supreme creative power, for the Cenozoic Era in the story of Earth is fading as the sunset in the western sky. Our hope for the future is for a new dawn, an Ecozoic Era, when humans will be present to the Earth in a mutually enhancing manner.

Dusk

A new language,
an Ecozoic language, is needed.

INVOCATION

We are listening to Earth tell its story
through the light that comes to us from the stars,
through its geological formations,
and through the vast amount of data
that the biosystems of Earth gives us.

DOXOLOGY

We are experiencing a moment of grace.
Such moments are privileged moments.
The great transformations of the universe occur at such times.
The present is one of those moments of transformation.

Opening Verse

The creative work of the emerging twenty-first century is the shaping of an Ecozoic era to succeed the Cenozoic era, which is presently in its terminal phase.

Hymn

The splendor of Earth
is in the variety of its land and its seas,
its life-forms and its atmospheric phenomena
constitute in color and sound and movement
that great symphonic content
which has inspired our sense of the divine,
given us our emotional and imaginative powers,
and evoked from us those entrancing insights
that have governed our more sublime moments.

Antiphon

The Great Self is the universe itself.

Psalm

We have many selves.
The great secret of existence is the secret or mystique
of discovering the unity between our smaller self and our
    Great Self.

The Great Self is the universe itself.
So that in discovering the universe we discover ourselves.
The whole universe has been required
to produce ourselves individually.

We are significant in that sense,
and we don't understand our individual self
until we are able to place ourselves within this larger context.
Why are scientists so drawn to experience the universe?
Well, it is the call of the Great Self to the small self,
and we cannot be at peace until we venture into this.

ANTIPHON II

The never-ending sequence of wonders is the key to life itself.

PSALM II

The wonderful thing about the Divine
is that it is endless discovery on discovery on discovery.

That this is endless is so important
because if you ever came to the end,
then the interest is gone, the discovery will be gone.

And that is to a large extent,
the key to a successful and fulfilling life—
keeping always the wonder of the child.

As life unfolds, mystery unfolds unto mystery
unto mystery unto mystery.
To be able to follow this and to experience
this never-ending sequence of wonders is the key to life itself.
It is a requisite for our fulfillment.

PSALM PRAYER

Prevent the destruction of the divine image as presented to us in the created world, prevent the wiping out of the source of our spiritual, intellectual, and aesthetic development, prevent the burning away of irreplaceable resources for foolish and ephemeral purposes.

EPISTLE

I might conclude with a reference to the Exodus symbol, which has exercised such great power over our Western civilization. We have always had a sense of transition. Progress supposedly is taking us from an undesirable situation to a kind of beatitude. So we might think of the transition from the terminal Cenozoic to the emerging Ecozoic as a kind of Exodus out of a period when humans are devastating the planet to a period when humans will begin to live on the Earth in a mutually enhancing manner.

There is a vast difference, however, in the case of this present transition, which is one not simply of the human but of the entire planet—its land, its air, its water, its biosystems, its human communities.

Responsory

We need a spirituality that emerges out of a reality deeper than ourselves, a spirituality that is as deep as the Earth process itself, a spirituality born out of the solar system and even out of the heavens beyond the solar system. For it is in the stars that the primordial elements take shape in both their physical and psychic aspects.

Canticle

There are cosmological and historical moments of grace
as well as religious moments of grace.

The present is one of those moments of transformation
that can be considered as a cosmological,
as well as a historical and a religious moment of grace.

Such a moment occurred when the star
out of which our solar system was born
collapsed in enormous heat,
scattering itself as fragments in the vast realms of space.

In the center of this star
the elements had been forming through a vast period of time
until in the final heat of this explosion
the hundred-some elements were present.

Only then could the sun, our star, give shape to itself
by gathering these fragments together with gravitational
    power
and then leaving some nine spherical shapes
sailing in elliptical paths around itself as planetary forms.

At this moment Earth too could take shape;
life could be evoked;
intelligence in its human form became possible.

This supernova event of a first- or second-generation star
could be considered a cosmological moment of grace,
a moment that determined the future possibilities
of the solar system, Earth, and of every form of life
that would ever appear on the Earth.

INTERCESSIONS

EVOCATION

We must feel that we are supported by that same process
that brought the Earth into being,
that power that spun the galaxies into space,
that lit the sun and brought the moon into its orbit.
Those same forces are still present;
indeed, we might feel their impact at this time
and understand that we are not isolated in the chill of space
with the burden of the future upon us
and without the aid of any other power.

We are supported by . . . that power
that spun the galaxies into space.

CLOSING PRAYER

We must go far beyond any transformation of contemporary culture. We must go back to the genetic imperative from which human cultures emerge originally and from which they can never be separated without losing their integrity and their survival capacity. We must invent, or reinvent, a sustainable human culture by a descent into our prerational, our instinctive, resources. What is needed is not transcendence but "inscendence," not the brain but the gene.

Dark

Breath Prayer

*Out of the primordial elements
the solar system and Earth took shape,
and out of Earth, ourselves.*

INVOCATION

Finally, a reversal has begun, and the reality and value of the interior subjective numinous aspect of the entire cosmic order is being appreciated as the basic condition in which the story makes sense at all.

Doxology

We are experiencing a moment of grace.
Such moments are privileged moments.
The great transformations of the universe occur at such
    times.
The present is one of those moments of transformation.

Opening Verse

The key to a successful and fulfilling life
is keeping always the wonder of the child.

Hymn

Discover for the first time
the integral community in which we live.
Experience the reality and the values
that evoke in us our deepest moments of reflection,
our revelatory experience
of the ultimate mystery of things.

Here, in this intimate presence to the valley in all its vitality,
we receive those larger intuitions that lead us to dance and
    sing,
intuitions that activate our imaginative powers
in their most creative functions.

This, too, is what inspires our weddings,
our home life, and our joy in our children.

Even our deepest human sensitivities
emerge from our region, our place, our specific habitat,
for the Earth does not give itself to us
in a global sameness.
It gives itself to us
in arctic and tropical regions,
in seashore and desert,
in prairie-lands and woodlands,
in mountains and valleys.

Out of each
a unique shaping of life takes place,
a community, an integral community
of all the geological as well as the biological
and the human components.

Each region is a single community so intimately related
that any benefit or any injury is immediately experienced
throughout the entire community.

Antiphon

Be sensitized to what is being revealed to us.

Psalm

A new revelatory experience is needed,
an experience wherein human consciousness awakens
to the grandeur and sacred quality of the Earth process.

This awakening is our human participation
in the dream of the Earth,
the dream that is carried in its integrity
not in any of Earth's cultural expressions
but in the depths of our genetic coding.

Therein the Earth functions at a depth
beyond our capacity for active thought.

We can only be sensitized
to what is being revealed to us.

Psalm Prayer

We have not had such participation in the dream of the Earth
since earlier shamanic times, but therein lies our hope for the
future for ourselves and for the entire Earth community.

~Silence~

LITANY

* As the crashing of the tropical rainforest resounds about us,
* as the sun is dimmed in the day and the stars at night by the hovering pollution in the atmosphere,
* as the great hydrological cycles are disturbed in their vast role of watering the continents and bringing forth the greenery of the land,
* as a multitude of living species become extinct throughout the Earth—

Even amid all these events, there is a resilience, a hope, and even an expectation for a surviving abundance of life upon Earth, if only the human community will respond to the urgency with insight and vigor.

CLOSING PRAYER

The basic mood of the future might well be one of confidence in the continuing revelation that takes place in and through the Earth. If the dynamics of the universe from the beginning shaped the course of the heavens, lighted the sun, and formed the Earth, if this same dynamism brought forth the continents and seas and atmosphere, if it awakened life in the primordial cell and then brought into being the unnumbered variety of living beings, and finally brought us into being and guided us safely through the turbulent centuries, there is reason to believe that this same guiding process is precisely what has awakened in us our present understanding of ourselves and our relation to this stupendous process. Sensitized to such guidance from the very structure and functioning of the universe, we can have confidence in the future that awaits the human venture.

Final Benediction

This Exodus is a journey of the Earth entire.
It is my hope that we will make the transition successfully.
Whatever the future holds for us, however,
it will be an experience shared
by humans and every other earthly being.
There is only one community, one destiny.
—Thomas Berry

Postscript

Kathleen Deignan, CND

Thomas Berry: to have known him in time was to be drawn to his humble, homey self—gracious beyond words, brilliant beyond belief. Yet clothed in his signature simplicity, the soft-spoken Southern gentleman, priest, and professor was a visionary mystic and fierce environmental prophet announcing to all who would hear, the dire circumstances yet vibrant potentials of our present Earth order.

About a year before Thomas passed in 2009, my colleague from the Deignan Institute for Earth and Spirit and I made a final visitation seeking the blessing of our revered teacher. Brother Kevin and I spent the next two days trying to keep up with our ninety-one-year-old mentor whose energy to continue teaching seemed boundless. But it was sunset now, and we were witnessing the waning of a great Earth prophet. Because we wished to be among his lineage bearers, I knelt before him to invoke a blessing on the "The Great Work" he was leaving us at this critical moment in Earth's history. With shy embarrassment, he made a vague sign of the cross before me and gently touched my cheek like a bishop confirming and commissioning. It was an intimate "moment of grace," an informal transmission of his spirit to ours to carry on—to carry *him* on—as two more among his many lineage bearers.

This empowering moment continues to bless all that our growing tribe of Berry Kin has since undertaken as a living memorial to him. Not long after that encounter, Thomas passed into the invisible universe he so illuminated with his prophetic and poetic voice. In his honor, my brothers Brian Brown, Kevin Cawley, Danny Martin, and I inaugurated The Thomas Berry Forum for Ecological Dialogue at Iona University to keep his inspired voice sounding as an evangelist of an age that is to come, if we so will it, if we would build it, embody it: the *Ecozoic*.

Long live our *house of life* and all Earthlings who abide therein. Long live the Berry Kin who labor to honor and protect it and who make up the friendship network sustaining us in the Great Work:

Green Mountain Monastery Sisters, Anthony Mullen, Carl and Elena Procario-Foley, Liam Myers, Vaughn Fayle, Scott Thompson, Kathy Duffy, Teresa Delgado, Joe Holland, Fletcher Harper and GreenFaith Fellows, Jackie Hanrahan, Libby Osgood, Maco Cassetta, Sam King, Monica Hoyt, Berry Forum Contemplative Ecologists, the Faculty of Religious Studies, Marie Pace, Joseph Stabile, and all my beloved Iona colleagues who teach the New Story and serve the Living Earth. May we all live in the spirit of its servant: Thomas Berry.

Abbreviations

CFFE   *The Christian Future and the Fate of Earth*

DE   *The Dream of the Earth*

EB   "Every Being Has Rights," Schumacher Lecture

EE   "The Ecozoic Era," Schumacher Lecture

ET   *Evening Thoughts*

LOYNO   *Reflections with Thomas Berry*:
http://cnh.loyno.edu/sites/default/files/ file_
attach/50th_earth_day_reflections_with_thomas_
berry.pdf

GW   *The Great Work*

SU   *The Sacred Universe*

TB   http://thomasberry.org

References

Prologue: "The Meadow Across the Creek"
https://thomasberry.org/the-meadow-across-the-creek/

Sunday Dawn
Breath Prayer, 22 in GW
Invocation, 31 in GW
Doxology, 70 in ET
Opening Verse, 124 in DE
Hymn, 171–172 in DE
Antiphon & Psalm, 132 in DE
Psalm Prayer, 57 in ET
Reading, xi in DE
Versicle, xi–xii in DE
Responsory, 55 in ET
Cosmic Canticle, 26–27 in GW
Evocation,174 in GW
Closing Prayer, 34 in ET

Sunday Day

Breath Prayer, 23 in ET
Invocation, 62 in ET
Doxology, 70 in ET
Exhortation, 5 in DE
Antiphon & Psalm, 57 in ET
Psalm Prayer, 44 in SU
Meditation, 122–123 in SU
Prayer, 27 in GW
Lesson, 199 in DE
Collect, 41 in ET
Examen, 20 in DE; 117 in ET; 51 in GW
Confession, 50–51in DE
Benediction, 114–115 in ET; 31–32 in GW

Sunday Dusk

Breath Prayer, 60 in ET
Invocation, xv in DE
Doxology, 70 in ET
Opening Verse, 45–46 in DE
Evening Hymn, 31 in ET
Antiphon & Psalm, 137 in ET
Antiphon & Psalm, 50 in GW
Psalm Prayer, 23 in ET
Epistle, 123 in DE
Responsory, 118 in SU
Cosmic Canticle, TB, https://thomasberry.org/it-takes-a-universe/

Evocation, 174 in GW
Closing Prayer, 38 in ET

Sunday Dark
Breath Prayer, 65 in ET
Invocation, 20 in ET
Doxology, 70 in ET
Opening Verse, 123 in ET
Night Hymn, 24 in DE
Antiphon & Night Psalm, 70–71 in ET
Psalm Prayer, 14 in DE
Litany, 73 in CFFE
Closing Prayer, 138 in ET

Monday Dawn
Breath Prayer, 5 in DE
Invocation, 2, 15 in DE
Doxology, 82 in DE
Opening Verse, 18 in DE
Hymn DE, 1 in DE
Antiphon & Psalm, 134–135 in DE
Psalm Prayer, 61 in GW
Reading, 20 in DE
Versicle, 74 in CFFE
Responsory, 11 in DE
Cosmic Canticle, 11 in DE
Evocation, 174 in GW
Closing Prayer, 11 in DE

Monday Day

Breath Prayer, 19 in DE
Invocation, 75 in SU
Doxology, 82 in DE
Exhortation, 21 in DE
Antiphon & Psalm, 176–177 in GW
Psalm Prayer, xiv in DE
Meditation, 39–40 in ET
Prayer, 134 in DE
Lesson, 50 in GW
Collect, 5 in DE
Examen, 20, 173 in DE
Confession, 2 in DE
Benediction, 58 in ET

Monday Dusk

Breath Prayer, 31 in ET
Invocation, xv in DE
Doxology, 82 in DE
Opening Verse, 3 in DE
Evening Hymn, 1 in DE
Antiphon & Psalm, 14 in GW
Antiphon & Psalm, 198 in DE
Psalm Prayer, 20 in ET
Epistle, 125, 21 in ET
Responsory, 4 in DE
Cosmic Canticle, 49 in ET
Evocation, 174 in GW
Closing Prayer, 20 in DE

Monday Dark

Breath Prayer, 15 in DE
Invocation, 149, 40 in ET
Doxology, 82 in DE
Opening Verse, 120 in DE
Night Hymn, 20 in GW
Antiphon & Night Psalm, 64 in ET
Psalm Prayer, xiv–xv in DE
Litany, 107 in DE
Closing Prayer, 141 in ET

Tuesday Dawn

Breath Prayer, 21 in DE
Invocation, 73 in SU
Doxology, 57 in GW
Opening Verse, 56 in GW
Hymn, 118 in ET
Antiphon & Psalm, 82 in DE
Psalm Prayer, 118 in SU
Reading, 11–12 in DE
Versicle, 62 in ET
Responsory, 16 in DE
Cosmic Canticle, 122–123 in SU
Evocation, 174 in GW
Closing Prayer, 106 in ET

Tuesday Day

Breath Prayer, 41 in ET
Invocation, 12 in DE

Doxology, 57 in GW
Exhortation, 99 in SU
Antiphon & Psalm, 37 in DE
Psalm Prayer, 13 in DE
Meditation, 19–20 in DE
Breath Prayer, 170 in GW
Lesson, 4–5 in DE
Collect, 135 in DE
Examen, 20 in DE & 22 in ET
Confession, 44 in DE
Benediction, 174 in DE

Tuesday Dusk
Breath Prayer, xii in DE
Invocation, 9 in DE
Doxology, 57 in GW
Opening Verse, 190 in GW
Evening Hymn, 165 in DE
Antiphon & Psalm, 47 in DE
Antiphon & Psalm, 197 in GW
Psalm Prayer, 32 in GW
Epistle, 30 in DE
Responsory, 95 in DE
Cosmic Canticle, 118 in ET
Evocation, 174 in GW
Closing Prayer, 34 in ET

Tuesday Dark
Breath Prayer, 165 in DE
Invocation, 165 in DE

Doxology, 57 in GW
Opening Verse, 165 in DE
Night Hymn, 219–220 in DE
Antiphon & Night Psalm, 91 in DE
Psalm Prayer, 220 in DE
Litany, 83 in ET
Closing Prayer, 12 in DE

Wednesday Dawn
Breath Prayer, 45 in DE
Invocation, 58 in ET
Doxology, 71 in SU
Opening Verse, 33 in ET
Hymn, 39 in ET
Antiphon & Psalm, 18 in ET
Psalm Prayer, 34 in ET
Reading, 106 in DE
Versicle, 120 in DE
Responsory, 15 in DE
Cosmic Canticle, 176–177 in SU
Evocation, 174 in GW
Closing Prayer, 12 in DE

Wednesday Day
Prayer, 75 in CFFE
Invocation, 199 in DE
Doxology, 71 in SU
Exhortation, 13 in DE
Antiphon & Psalm, 178 in DE
Psalm Prayer, 145 in DE

Meditation, 48–49 in GW
Prayer, 9 in CFFE
Lesson, 5 in GW
Collect, 5 in GW
Examen, 20 &, 24 in GW
Confession, 2 in DE
Benediction, 23 in DE

WEDNESDAY DUSK
Breath Prayer, xiii in DE
Invocation, 71 in SU
Doxology, 71 in SU
Opening Verse, 71 in SU
Evening Hymn, 117 in ET
Antiphon & Psalm, https://centerforneweconomics.org/
    publications/every-being-has-rights/
Antiphon & Psalm, 16 in DE
Psalm Prayer, 174 in GW
Epistle, 6 in DE
Responsory, 173–74 in GW
Cosmic Canticle, 174–175 in GW
Evocation, 174 in GW
Closing Prayer, 177 in DE

WEDNESDAY DARK
Breath Prayer, xiv in DE
Invocation, 174 in GW
Doxology, 71 in SU
Opening Verse, 174 in GW

Night Hymn, 47 in DE
Antiphon & Night Psalm, 91 in DE
Psalm Prayer, 149 in GW
Litany, 138 in ET
Closing Prayer, 61 in GW

THURSDAY DAWN

Prayer, 3 in DE
Invocation, 1 in GW
Doxology, 25–26 in DE
Opening Verse, 71 in SU
Hymn, 14 in DE
Antiphon & Psalm, 20 in GW
Psalm Prayer, 15 in GW
Reading, 216–217 in DE
Versicle, 35 in DE
Responsory, 19 in GW
Cosmic Canticle, 222–223 in DE
Evocation, 174 in GW
Closing Prayer, 11 in GW

THURSDAY DAY

Breath Prayer, 71 in SU
Invocation, 10 in GW
Doxology, 25–26 in DE
Exhortation, 47 in SU
Antiphon & Psalm, 20, 17 in GW
Psalm Prayer, 41 in ET
Meditation, 60 in ET & 10 in CFFE

Prayer, 162 in GW
Lesson, 43 in DE
Collect, 71 & 47 in DE
Examen, 20 in DE & 39–40 in ET
Confession, 17 in GW
Benediction, 195 in GW

Thursday Dusk
Breath Prayer, 54 in GW
Invocation, 177 in DE
Doxology, 25, 26 in DE
Opening Verse, 36 in DE
Evening Hymn, 69 in DE
Antiphon & Psalm, 123 in ET
Antiphon & Psalm, 32–33 in DE
Psalm Prayer, 37 in DE
Epistle, 37, 42 in DE
Responsory, 42 in DE
Cosmic Canticle, https://thomasberry.org/every-being-has-rights/
Evocation, 174 in GW
Closing Prayer, 79 in DE

Thursday Dark
Breath Prayer, 162 in GW
Invocation, 2 in CFFE
Doxology, 25 in DE
Opening Verse, 39 in ET
Night Hymn, 200–201 in GW

Antiphon & Night Psalm, 21 in GW
Psalm Prayer, 21 in GW
Litany, 34 in ET
Closing Prayer, 175 in GW

Friday Dawn
Breath Prayer, 209 in DE
Invocation, 194–195 in DE
Doxology, 49 in GW
Opening Verse, 11 in DE
Hymn, 117 in CFFE
Antiphon & Psalm, 119 in DE
Psalm Prayer, 15 in GW
Reading, https://thomasberry.org/the-ecozoic-era/
Versicle, https://thomasberry.org/the-ecozoic-era/
Responsory, 117 in CFFE
Cosmic Canticle, xiv in DE
Evocation, 174 in GW
Closing Prayer, 2 in DE

Friday Day
Breath Prayer, 9 in DE
Invocation, 73–74 in CFFE
Doxology, 49 in GW
Exhortation, 7–8 in DE
Antiphon & Psalm, 15 in GW
Psalm Prayer, 204 in DE
Meditation, 8 in DE &, 73–74
Prayer, 48 in SU

Lesson, 10–11 in DE & https://thomasberry.org/the-ecozoic-era/

Collect, 10 in CFFE

Examen, 20, 16–17 in DE

Confession, 14–15 in SU

Benediction, 222 in DE

FRIDAY DUSK
Breath Prayer, 175 in SU

Invocation, 98 in CFFE

Doxology, 49 in GW

Opening Verse, 29 in DE

Evening Hymn, 66 in ET

Antiphon & Psalm, 10 in DE

Antiphon & Psalm, 209 in DE

Psalm Prayer, 15 in DE

Epistle, 9 in SU

Responsory, 15 in SU

Cosmic Canticle, https://thomasberry.org/morningside-cathedral/

Evocation, 174 in GW

Closing Prayer, 42 in CFFE

FRIDAY DARK
Breath Prayer, 36 in DE

Invocation, 14 in SU

Doxology, 49 in GW

Opening Verse, 18 in DE

Night Hymn DE, 194 in DE

Antiphon & Night Psalm, 90 in ET
Psalm Prayer, 10 in CFFE
Litany DE, 9 in DE
Closing Prayer, 7 in CFFE

SATURDAY DAWN
Breath Prayer, 46 in SU
Invocation, 76–77 in SU
Doxology, 46 in SU
Opening Verse, 118 in SU
Hymn, 5 in DE
Antiphon & Psalm, 81 in DE
Psalm Prayer, 71 in SU
Reading, 170 in SU
Versicle, 220 in DE
Responsory, 198 in DE
Cosmic Canticle, https://thomasberry.org/an-appalachian-wedding/
Evocation, 174 in GW
Closing Prayer, 98 in CFFE

SATURDAY DAY
Breath Prayer, 162 in DE
Invocation, 116 in CFFE
Doxology, 46 in SU
Exhortation, 161–162 in DE
Antiphon & Psalm, 1 in CFFE
Psalm Prayer, 34 in DE
Meditation, 38 in SU

Prayer DE, 162 in DE
Lesson, 46 in SU
Collect, 170 in GW
Examen, 20 in DE & 117 in ET
Confession, 130 in DE &, 173 in SU
Benediction, 195 in DE

SATURDAY DUSK
Breath Prayer, 121 in DE
Invocation, 116 in ET
Doxology, 46 in SU
Opening Verse, 219–220 in DE
Evening Hymn, https://thomasberry.org/earths-desire/
Antiphon & Psalm, 139 in ET
Antiphon & Psalm, 67–68 in GW
Psalm Prayer, 139 in ET
Epistle, 69 in SU
Responsory, 172 in SU
Cosmic Canticle, 139 in ET
Evocation, 174 in GW
Closing Prayer, 87 in SU

SATURDAY DARK
Breath Prayer, 120–121 in DE
Invocation, 87 in DE
Doxology, 46 in SU
Opening Verse, 70 in GW
Night Hymn, 163 in DE
Antiphon & Night Psalm, 32 in GW

Psalm Prayer, in DE 195
Litany, 170 in SU
Closing Prayer, 222–223 in DE

Toward the Ecozoic Dawn

Breath Prayer, 43 in SU
Invocation, 43 in SU
Doxology, 196 in GW
Opening Verse, 46 in DE
Hymn, 46 in DE
Antiphon & Psalm, 197 in DE
Psalm Prayer, 198 in DE
Reading, 121 in DE
Versicle, 82 in SU
Responsory, 11 in CFFE
Cosmic Canticle, https://thomasberry.org/the-gravitation/
Evocation, 174 in GW
Closing Prayer, 211 in DE

Toward the Ecozoic Day

Prayer, 25–26 in DE
Invocation, 135 in SU
Doxology, 196 in GW
Exhortation, 43 in SU
Antiphon & Psalm
http://cnh.loyno.edu/sites/default/files/file_attach/50th_
    earth_day_reflections_with_thomas_berry.pdf
Psalm Prayer, 23 in SU
Meditation, 175 in SU

Prayer, https://thomasberry.org/the-ecozoic-era/
Lesson, 59–60 in SU
Collect, 135–136 in SU
Examen, 20, 43 in DE
Confession, xiii in DE
Benediction, 55 in GW

Toward the Ecozoic Dusk

Breath Prayer in EE
Invocation, 118 in SU
Doxology, 196 in GW
Opening Verse, 60 in ET
Evening Hymn, 165 in DE
Antiphon & Psalm
http://cnh.loyno.edu/sites/default/files/file_attach/50th_
    earth_day_reflections_with_thomas_berry.pdf
Antiphon & Psalm
http://cnh.loyno.edu/sites/default/files/file_attach/50th_
    earth_day_reflections_with_thomas_berry.pdf
Psalm Prayer, 10 in CFFE
Epistle, https://thomasberry.org/the-ecozoic-era/
Responsory, 74 in SU
Cosmic Canticle, 196 in GW
Evocation, 174 in GW
Closing Prayer, 207–208 in DE

Toward the Ecozoic Dark

Breath Prayer, 74 in SU
Invocation, 135 in DE

Doxology, 96 in GW
Opening Verse
http://cnh.loyno.edu/sites/default/files/file_attach/50th_
earth_day_reflections_with_thomas_berry.pdf
Night Hymn, 176 in DE
Antiphon & Night Psalm, 165 in GW
Psalm Prayer, 165 in GW
Litany, xiii–xiv in DE
Closing Prayer, 137 in DE

FINAL BENEDICTION
https://thomasberry.org/the-ecozoic-era/

Bibliography and Permissions

The Christian Future and the Fate of Earth. Edited by Mary Evelyn Tucker and John Grim. Maryknoll, NY: Orbis Books, 2009. Excerpts reprinted with permission of Orbis Books.

The Dream of the Earth. Berkeley: Counterpoint Press, 2015. (Orig. San Francisco: Sierra Club Books, 1988.) Copyright © 1988 by Thomas Berry. Excerpts reprinted with the permission of The Permissions Company, LLC, on Behalf of Counterpoint Press, counterpointpress.com.

Evening Thoughts: Reflecting on Earth as Sacred Community. Edited by Mary Evelyn Tucker. Berkeley: Counterpoint Press, 2015. (Orig. San Francisco: Sierra Club Books & University of California Press, 2006.) Copyright © 2016 by Thomas Berry. Excerpts reprinted with the permission of The Permissions Company, LLC, on Behalf of Counterpoint Press, counterpointpress.com.

The Great Work: Our Way into the Future. New York: Harmony/Bell Tower, 1999.

The Sacred Universe: Earth, Spirituality, and Religion in the Twenty-First Century. Edited by Mary Evelyn Tucker. New York: Columbia University Press, 2009. Excerpts reprinted with permission of Columbia University Press.

Thomas Berry: A Biography. By Mary Evelyn Tucker, John Grim, and Andrew Angyal. New York: Columbia University Press, 2019.